A2 Religious Studies

advancing learning, changing lives

A2 Religious Studies

Sarah K. Tyler
Gordon Reid

Jon Mayled

Dominique Messent

Jennifer Uzzell-Smith

Published by:
Pearson Education Limited
Edinburgh Gate
Harlow
Essex CM20 2JE

First published 2009
10 9 8

ISBN 978-1-84690-494-3

Cover and book design by Rupert Purcell
Page make-up by Bob Vickers
Picture research by Susan Millership
Project management by Jayne de Courcy and Will Burrows
Production by Carol Gunn
Printed in Malaysia CTP-PJB

Picture credits
The publishers would like to thank the following for permission to reproduce copyright material:
p3 © (top) TopFoto / HIP (bottom) Roger-Viollet / Topfoto; p6 © TopFoto / ImageWorks; pp 14, 16
© Topham Picturepoint / TopFoto; p20 © World History Archive / TopFoto; p22 © TopFoto; p33
© 2002 Topham Picturepoint; p32 © 2005 TopFoto; p35 © Lalla Ward; p36 © Russ Mackechnie;
pp 45, 46, 47 © TopFoto; p50 © 2005 Charles Walker / TopFoto; p54 © TopFoto / HIP; p57
© Topham / Feltz; p59 © 2006 Alinari / TopFoto; p62 © 2003 Topham Picturepoint; p64 © 2006
TopFoto / Marie-Louise Avery; pp69, 71 © 2003 Topham Picturepoint; p78 © 2006 Alinari /
TopFoto; p80 © 2005 TopFoto / ImageWorks; p87 © Envision / Corbis; p92 © Print Collector / HIP /
TopFoto; p93 © TopFoto; © Etienne Ansotte / epa / Corbis; p94 © Etienne Ansotte / epa / Corbis;
p96 © 1999 Topham Picturepoint; pp100, 102 © 2006 TopFoto / Keystone; p103 © 2005 TopFoto /
EMPICS; p106 © 2002 Topham / PA; pp114, 118, 123 © 2004 TopFoto / ImageWorks; p117
© EMPICS / TopFoto; p121 © 2004 TopFoto / UPP
Cover image © Alamy Images/ Larry Mulvehill

Contents

Introduction   vi

Philosophy of Religion

Chapter 1   Philosophical arguments about the existence of God   1

   1.1   Religious experiences   1

   1.2   The ontological argument   15

   1.3   Atheism and critiques of religious belief   27

Chapter 2   Selected problems in the philosophy of religion   43

   2.1   Life after death   43

   2.2   Religious language   60

Ethics

Chapter 3   Ethical concepts   73

   3.1   Critiques of the relationship between religion and morality   73

   3.2   Ethical theory   83

Chapter 4   Selected problems in ethics   99

   4.1   Ethical language   99

   4.2   Objectivity, subjectivism and relativism   111

   4.3   Justice, law and punishment   116

Index   124

Introduction to Edexcel A2 Religious Studies

About the exam

The A2 exam revolves around two units – Unit 3: Developments and Unit 4: Implications. Both Unit 3 and Unit 4 are assessed by a written exam. In the Unit 3 exam you will be required to answer three questions from a choice of thirty-six, covering nine possible areas of study, of which you must study *at least* two. The nine areas of study are:

- Philosophy of Religion
- Ethics
- Buddhism
- Christianity
- Hinduism
- Islam
- Judaism
- Sikhism
- New Testament.

Four questions will be set on each area of study, consisting of two either/or options. In the Unit 4 exam, you will be required to choose one passage of text to discuss, responding to a single, generic question. One passage is set per area of study.

About this book

This book contains the content required by the specification for two areas of study: Philosophy of Religion and Ethics.

There are 'Test Yourself questions' at the end of sections within a chapter. These are denoted by this icon in the margin:

The questions – and sample answers – are on the accompanying CD-ROM.

About the CD-ROM

The CD-ROM contains the content for the other seven areas of study – Buddhism, Christianity, Hinduism, Islam, Judaism, Sikhism, and New Testament – as well as Philosophy of Religion and Ethics. There is also exam guidance for each area and guidance on Unit 4: Implications.

The initial screen on the CD-ROM allows you to select any one of the nine areas of study. You can then decide whether to view the content on screen, go straight to the 'Test Yourself questions' or print off the whole module. (The print option is not available for Philosophy of Religion and Ethics as these are in the textbook.)

The CD-ROM also contains the full AS/A2 specification in printable form.

CHAPTER 1
Philosophical arguments about the existence of God

1.1 Religious experiences

Key Ideas

- What is a religious experience?

- Types of religious experience

- Factors that lead to religious experiences

- Arguments in favour of religious experiences

- Arguments against religious experiences

- Is it meaningful to talk about religious experiences?

What is a religious experience?

A religious experience is an encounter with the divine. It is a non-empirical occurrence that brings with it an awareness of something beyond ourselves. For believers, this makes religious experience the most convincing proof of the existence of God. Saint Teresa of Avila described it thus: 'God establishes himself in the interior of this soul in such a way, that when I return to myself, it is wholly impossible for me to doubt that I have been in God and God in me.'

The variety of religious experiences is such that it is difficult to find a common theme. However, it is possible to divide them into two basic groups – a **direct experience**, where the person having the experience (the experient) feels that he or she is in contact with God, and an **indirect experience**, where there is an inner experience of God's action in creation (immanence) and 'something other'. In *The Evidential Force of Religious Experience* (Clarendon, 1989), Caroline Franks Davis suggests the following seven types of religious experience:

- seeing the work of God when looking at the world (**awareness** experience)
- having a vision or other inner experience of God (**quasi-sensory** experience)
- encountering the holiness of God (**numinous** experience)
- a conversion experience (**regenerative** experience)
- having prayers answered (**interpretive** experience)

- a sense of the ultimate reality (**mystical** experience)
- receiving enlightenment and knowledge, perhaps through a revelation from God (**revelatory** experience).

Every testimony of a religious experience is unique. Most occur to individuals in private, but others are 'corporate' experiences, when a large number of people share the same experience, such as the Toronto Blessing (see page 6). The majority of testimonies, however, reveal certain common themes. In *Sociology of the Paranormal* (Sage, 1975), Andrew Greeley surveys a large number of testimonies in the USA, discovering that the most common themes coming from religious experiences are:

- a feeling of deep, inner peace
- a certainty that everything will turn out for the good
- a sense of the need to help others
- a belief that love is at the centre of everything
- a sense of joy
- great emotional intensity.

Scholars have made various attempts to define what a religious experience actually is. Ninian Smart, in *The Religious Experience of Mankind* (Fontana, 1969), wrote that 'A religious experience involves some kind of 'perception' of the invisible world, or a perception that some visible person or thing is a manifestation of the invisible world.' Edward Schleiermacher, in *On Religion: Speeches to its Cultured Despisers*, defines a religious experience as one that offers a sense of the ultimate and an awareness of wholeness, a consciousness of the infinite and an absolute dependence.

Martin Buber, in *I and Thou* (New York, 1970), argues that God reveals himself to people on a personal level as they experience him in life and in the world – in other words, people experience God through interaction with other people and through nature. He wrote that everyday human relationships are normally on a simple level, what he calls '*I-It*'. However, serious and more meaningful relationships go much deeper, what he calls '*I-Thou*'. He argues that it is in such relationships that we experience God – he is 'the Eternal Thou'.

Paul Tillich, in *Systematic Theology* (Nisbet, 1951), states that a religious experience is a feeling of 'ultimate concern', a feeling that demands a decisive decision from the one receiving it. He describes it as an encounter, followed by a special understanding of its religious significance. *The New Dictionary of Theology* (ed. S. Fergusen and D. Wright, IVP, 1988) observes: 'Religious experience without religious reflection is blind, every claim to an experience of God requires examination… Christianity has no concept of religious experiences that do not have doctrinal or ethical consequences, or of experiences of God that do not involve a human response…'

Williams James, in *Varieties of Religious Experience* (Penguin, ed. 1983), observes that religious experiences draw on the common range of emotions, notably happiness, fear and wonder — but that they are directed at the divine. This gives the person an overwhelming feeling of reverence, a joyful desire to belong to God, a renewed approach to life: 'God was present, though invisible; he fell under not one of my senses, yet my consciousness perceived him.'

Taking it further...

Schleiermacher argues that the most significant factor in a religious experience is that it is based not on religious doctrine, but on faith and real human experience. Further, he suggests that all the world's religions offer part of the greater picture – from Christianity comes the sense of infinity and incarnation, from Islam the majesty and sovereignty of God, and from Judaism the law and morality of God.

Taking it further...

Three steps of preparation for religious experience have been identified:
- **purgation** – ridding the soul of tendencies that prevent it from paying attention
- **illumination** – preliminary disclosures which focus attention
- **contemplation** – the stage in which the presence of the divine penetrates the believer.

Richard Dawkins, in *The God Delusion* (Bantam, 2006), even claims that there is no such thing as a religious experience – they are merely expressions of a person's psychological needs: 'The argument from personal experience is the one that is the most convincing to those who claim to have had one. But it is the least convincing to anyone else, especially anyone knowledgeable about psychology.'

Saint Teresa of Avila before the Cross

Taking it further...

Even the great Christian mystic **Saint Teresa of Avila**, who had received so many profound visions, found it impossible to define a religious experience: 'I wish I could give a description of at least the smallest part of what I learned, but, when I try to discover a way of doing so, I find it impossible…'

Types of religious experience

1 The dramatic or conversion event

This is considered a direct experience, described by Rudolf Otto in *The Idea of the Holy* (OUP, 1923) as the **numinous** (from the Latin *numen,* meaning divinity). It refers to a religious experience that offers evidence of the 'wholly other' nature of God. Often the person sees a vision, accompanied by feelings of awe, wonder and humility before the power and majesty of God. It may sometimes be a conversion experience, such as that of Paul on the road to Damascus (Acts 9), in which the experient converts from one faith to another. Frequently, it is linked to a search for faith, a sense of guilt and sin, and communication from God involving reassurance and a feeling of certainty. John Wesley described such an experience: 'I felt my heart strangely warmed. I felt I did trust in Christ, Christ alone, for salvation; and an assurance was given me, that He had taken away my sins, even mine…' (Brian Davies, *An Introduction to the Philosophy of Religion*, Oxford University Press, 1982).

Taking it further...

Rudolph Otto claims that the numinous is a mysterious, but nevertheless real object of experience, which evokes feelings of awe, wonder and fascination. This experience of the holy is not the result of rational thinking but comes directly from intuition – people just 'know' that God is there.

In such experiences, the individual is both attracted and repelled by a sense of awe and wonder: 'Depart from me, for I am a sinful man, O Lord' (Luke 5:8); 'Woe is me! For I am lost; for I am a man of unclean lips, and I dwell in the midst of a people of unclean lips; for my eyes have seen the King, the Lord of hosts' (Isaiah 6:5).

2 Responses to life and the world

These are gentler, indirect experiences, which enhance a person's understanding of their life and the world around them. They often come as a result of prayer or other communication with God, when believers claim that God guides them and helps them to make sense of their lives and the world. H.D. Lewis claimed that it was 'Not just a feeling… but a conviction or insight, a sense that something must be'.

3 Revelatory experiences

Revelation is divine self-disclosure. It is a particular experience where God makes himself directly known, for example by a vision or dream. One crucial aspect of a revelatory experience is that the experient acquires new

The Transfiguration, *fresco by Fra Angelico* (1387–1455)

knowledge – for instance, universal truths about God, the future or a prophecy. There are two types:

- **Propositional revelation**, in which God communicates his divine message to a human being, for example Moses receiving the Ten Commandments or Muhammad receiving the Qur'an
- **Non-propositional revelation**, in which, through religious experience, a person comes to a moment of 'realisation' of divine truth, for instance when the Buddha gained enlightenment.

Taking it further...

Peter Cole, in *Religious Experience* (Hodder, 2005), cites the example of the world-famous preacher Benny Hinn as someone who claimed a revelatory experience. In front of a crowd of 18,000 people in 1993, he declared:

The Lord spoke to me… before you leave this stadium tonight, every person here will receive a fresh flowing of God's power on your life, and you are going to see demons bow when you say, 'in the name of Jesus of Nazareth'…

For the sceptic, such claims are virtually impossible to verify, and are easily open to accusations of fraud.

---

4 Near-death experiences

A near-death experience is said to occur when a person 'dies', usually in a medical operation, and is later resuscitated and can recall the experience of what happened to him/her when they 'died'. Extensive research on this phenomenon was carried out by Raymond Moody in his work *Life after Life* (Mockingbird, 1975). He looked at many such cases and found a number of 'core experiences' that seemed to be common to most. These included a feeling of peace and ineffability, going through a dark tunnel, meeting a being of light and having to make a decision about whether or not to cross a barrier before returning to life. But is a near-death experience a religious experience? Certainly they share common ground, such as the feeling of peace and ineffability, and many religious believers claim that the being of light is Jesus, Muhammad or God. Many scriptures apparently support the evidence:

And I know that this man – whether in the body or apart from the body I do not know, but God knows – was caught up to paradise (2 Corinthians 12:4).

The divine being of clear light will appear in whatever shape will benefit all beings (Tibetan Book of the Dead).

Not surprisingly, those who have had such an experience claim that it proves without doubt that there is life after death and that God exists.

5 Mystical experiences

A mystical experience is one in which a person experiences the ultimate reality, which brings with it a sense of unity with the divine, separateness from the divine and dependence on the divine. This is an experience which often proves difficult to describe in ordinary language. It is a category within the broader context of religious experience in which one is overwhelmingly swept up in the presence of God. It is intensely personal, other-worldly and transcendent;

an experience in which the recipient in some way touches and communicates with the divine and with levels of reality beyond those of the spatio-temporal world. The famous mystic **Saint John of the Cross** observed: 'Human language is unable to express the sense of mystical union with God'. Attempts to define a mystic experience include the following:

> *The Christian mystic is regarded as one who has been raised to a high degree of contemplative prayer. The mystical experience consists in a conscious, deep and intimate union of the soul with God... while the soul, on its part, has prepared itself, normally according to an accepted pattern of asceticism.* (Clifton Wolters (Introduction to) *Revelations of Divine Love*, Penguin Books Ltd, June 1982)

> *... joy supreme comes to the Yogi whose heart is still, whose passions are at peace, who is pure from sin, who is one with Brahman, with God* (Bhagavad Gita).

Sufism is the inner, mystical aspect of Islam and Sufis believe that it is possible, through meditative and other techniques, to become close to God: 'Adorn me with Thy Unity, clothe me with the Selfhood and raise me up to thy Oneness...' (Abu Yazid, cited in *Hindu and Muslim Mysticism* (Oneworld, 1994).

One of the most famous British mystics was Mother Julian of Norwich. She received 16 'showings' on 8 May 1373, during a time of dire sickness. Although she describes herself as 'uneducated', her evaluations of these showings are insightful and profound.

> *Our Lord showed me a little thing, the quantity of a hazelnut, in the palm of my hand; and it was as round as a ball. I looked thereupon with the eye of my understanding, and thought: 'What may this be?' And it was answered generally thus: 'It is all that is made'. I marvelled how it might last, for methought it might suddenly have fallen to naught for littleness. And I was answered in my understanding: 'It lastest and ever shall last for that God loveth it. And so All-thing hath Being by the love of God. In this Little Thing I saw three properties. The first is that God made it, the second that God loveth it, the third that God keepeth it.*

Although experiences of this kind are virtually impossible to verify, Clifton Wolters (ibid.) observes: 'Only if we deny any possibility of divine communication can Julian's claims be completely ruled out...'

There are two types of mysticism, **theistic mysticism**, which involves an awareness of God, and **monistic mysticism**, which offers awareness of the soul, self and conscience. In *The Varieties of Religious Experience* (Penguin, 1983), William James lists the four characteristics of mystic experiences thus:

- **ineffability** – a state of feeling that defies description

- **noetic quality** – revelations of universal and eternal truths

- **transiency** – a brief but profoundly important experience

- **passivity** – a feeling of being taken over by a superior authority.

Mysticism can be both **extrovertive**, looking outwards to see God in the world, or **introvertive**, where the person looks within themselves and sees their personal identity being merged into the divine unity. According to Hans Kung in *Does God Exist?* (London, 1980), mysticism is characterised by a

Taking it further...

William James concludes that these feelings prove that something really has happened. He accepts that there may be other physiological symptoms involved as well, but says that these should not detract from the fact that the person receives an experience of something beyond themselves: 'The results of religious experience are the only reliable basis for judging whether it is a genuine experience of the divine' (ibid.).

closing of the senses to the outside world and a dissolving of the self. It is an individual experience, whereby the person seeks a loving union with God by purifying their own soul.

6 Corporate experiences

In January 1994, a series of corporate religious experiences known as the Toronto Blessing originated at the Airport Vineyard Church in Toronto, with large numbers of people seeming to experience God at the same time. People shook uncontrollably, wept, laughed hysterically and made unusual sounds like the barking of dogs. The Airport Vineyard Church had often had incidents of charismatic worship and manifestations of the Spirit, usually in the form of glossolalia [speaking in tongues] or prophecies, but had not before witnessed the holy laughter seen that evening. The Toronto Blessing has spread all over the USA and Canada and was brought to the United Kingdom by members of Holy Trinity Church, Brompton, London. Some people see the experience of the blessing as the hallmark of a true Christian church. Others have questioned its validity as a religious experience, claiming that the experiences are engineered through mass hysteria and the use of presentation technology.

Factors that lead to religious experiences

Scholars have generally accepted that certain conditions can trigger religious experiences. Andrew Greeley's research (ibid.) suggested that some of the most common triggers of religious experiences are music (and dance), prayer and meditation.

Music and atmosphere

A woman praises God during worship at the Springfield Baptist Church in Beacon, USA. A religious experience or crowd manipulation?

Most religions use music in worship. It offers a way for people to express their shared beliefs together and this can produce a communal and social experience that stirs people's hearts and minds. Dance, too, can be an expression of religious faith, joy and devotion — one of the most famous examples is the 'whirling dervishes' of the Sufi tradition in Islam. Within charismatic Christianity, the work of evangelists who lead massive crusades, often claiming to be the vehicle through which God performs miracles, is highly dependent on music and atmosphere generating the right circumstances in which those in a high state of expectation feel that they receive religious experiences. Perhaps the most famous exponent currently is Benny Hinn who, as well as conducting vast 'miracle crusades', has a daily programme on Trinity Network Broadcasting called *This is Your Day* and is the author of many bestselling books, including *Good Morning Holy Spirit.* He is a very controversial figure and many well-known and respected Christian writers and preachers speak out strongly against him and his claims, whilst others are hugely supportive of him.

Benny Hinn was born in Israel to a Greek father and Armenian mother and was raised in the Greek Orthodox faith. However, when the family moved to Canada, he was born again. He received many visions of him preaching before huge crowds, and he has continued to claim many experiences where God has spoken to him directly and has made clear the very special role that God has for him. Hinn's critics have apparently identified many inconsistencies in the information that he has given about his early life and have strongly criticised his teaching which, they claim, is often based on false understandings of the Bible, although Hinn has often claimed special 'revelation knowledge' – that is, God making something new known to him.

Hinn was strongly influenced by miracle workers of the 1960s and 1970s, especially by Kathryn Kulmann, who carried out miracle crusades and attracted thousands of followers. He was particularly impressed by the technique she adopted of encouraging people to fall down, apparently under the power of the Holy Spirit. This is called being 'slain in the Spirit' and looks very dramatic when it happens on stage. Hinn blows on willing volunteers or pushes them over with the exclamation 'Substance!', knocking them down again when Hinn's helpers get them to their feet. Critics claim that this has nothing to do with the power of God, but is a hypnotic technique used to persuade people to fall by the power of suggestion. Critics also feel that some of Hinn's own staff fall simply as part of Hinn's act. It creates an atmosphere of excitement and expectation amongst the crowd, who then believe anything is possible – including the paralysed getting out of their wheelchairs.

Prayer

Prayer is communion with God. It comes in many forms, including prayers of thanks, of asking for help and guidance, for forgiveness and for praise. Believers claim that God answers prayers and that this is a sure sign of his existence. Archbishop William Temple observed: 'When I pray, coincidences happen, and when I don't, they don't.'

One particular type of prayer involves the phenomenon known as 'speaking in tongues' (**glossolalia**), where a person speaks, during prayer, in a language that is not known to them. This is given to the recipient by God as a sign of their 'Baptism of the Holy Spirit' – proof that God lives within them. It is most commonly found in the Charismatic Movement and the Pentecostal Church.

Meditation

In the theistic tradition, this is a prayerful state where a person seeks understanding of, and union with, God. In the non-theistic tradition, such as Buddhism, the aim is to seek the loss of self.

Arguments in favour of religious experiences as proof for the existence of God

The argument citing religious experience as proof of God's existence is an *a posteriori* one (derived from factual evidence); over the centuries, there have been many thousands of testimonies to religious experience. Such an argument is based on the premise that experience is, in some way, the product of facts about the real world. It could, for example, be set out in premises as follows:

- Premise 1: Experience of X indicates the reality of X.
- Premise 2: Experience of God indicates the reality of God.
- Premise 3: It is possible to experience God.
- Conclusion: God exists (i.e. is really present).

Taking it further...

For believers, religious experiences are not random occurrences. They play a crucial part in the lives of religious believers. Most agree that testimonies of such experiences need to be examined and reflected on carefully – a religious experience is a message from God that requires a response from the believer. Such experiences should be in keeping with the character of God and should have made a noticeable difference in the life of the person receiving the experience.

Unsurprisingly, there are considerable problems about this form of the argument. Firstly, it is clear that experience of X does not always indicate the reality of X. Our regular experience can easily be mistaken, and we are open to reassessing what we believe we have experienced. Premise 1 may therefore be better expressed as: 'Experience of X indicates the *probable* reality of X'. Premise 2 creates further problems, since if regular experience is open to misapprehension, then experience of the divine must be potentially even more ambiguous, given that it depends on appealing to non-empirical as well as empirical evidence. If we allow that regular experience indicates the *probable* reality of X, then experience of God must also indicate the *probable* reality of God, but it would be reasonable to suggest it is at a lower level of probability still.

Premise 3 takes the implications of Premise 2 a stage further. However, to say that it is 'possible' to experience God is ambiguous. Does it mean that it is possible that someone may claim to have experienced God, or that if God exists it is possible that he may be experienced? Is it possible to experience God in the way that we experience other human beings, trees or buses (that is, it is possible because we *do* have that experience) or is it possible to experience God in the way that we may experience unicorns (it is possible that they may or may not be experienceable)? Our knowledge of the world tells us that this possibility has so far not been realised, but it is not, in principle, discounted. In other words, Premise 3 does not tell us that experience of God has actually taken place, simply that under certain circumstances (which are themselves undefined), it is possible that God might be experienced.

The conclusion therefore cannot be sustained simply on the basis of the claims made in the premises. The most that can be claimed is that *if* experience is reliable, it can indicate the reality of that which is experienced, but this itself cannot be guaranteed. The most the premises amount to is a tentatively probable conclusion that God exists.

The inductive argument

The form of the argument outlined above is **inductive**, and those who believe that religious experiences are proof of the existence of God usually argue inductively. This means that they look at the subjective testimonies of individuals who claim to have had religious experiences, in order to find similar characteristics, and then draw the general conclusion that the experiences can only be explained in terms of the existence of God. Thus, Richard Swinburne in *Is there a God?* (Oxford University Press, 1996) argues inductively that it is reasonable to believe that God is loving and personal and would seek to reveal himself to humanity as an act of love and to enable people to bring about the good: 'An omnipotent and perfectly good creator will seek to interact with his creatures and, in particular, with human persons capable of knowing him'.

Swinburne is suggesting that religious experiences can be felt empirically — through our senses — and interpreted non-empirically, through our 'religious sense'. Thus, if we are told that someone has had a religious experience, then we should believe that experience has taken place, even if someone else has had a different experience or no experience at all. Brian Davies, in *Philosophy of Religion* (Oxford University Press, 2000), writes: 'We certainly do make

Taking it further...

Psychologist Carl Jung commented: 'Religious experience is absolute… it cannot be disputed. Those who have had it possess a great treasure, a source of life, meaning and beauty which gives splendour to the world.'

mistakes about reality because we fail to interpret our experience correctly; but if we do not work on the assumption that what seems to be so is sometimes so, then it is hard to see how we can establish anything at all…'.

Supporters of this view argue that the proof of religious experiences lies in the fact that the lives of those who experience them are changed forever. Moreover, some of the greatest events in history have resulted from people having religious experiences. For example:

- Paul was converted after seeing a vision of Christ and was instrumental in spreading Christianity around the known world.
- The Prophet Muhammad, the Buddha and Guru Nanak became the founders of their faiths after religious experiences.
- Joan of Arc led the French armies to victory after receiving a series of visions.

Nevertheless, the continued problem remains, which is applicable to any inductive argument: the conclusion is the best that appears probable on the basis of the evidence offered. However, the conclusion depends on an accurate interpretation of that evidence which may be inevitably influenced by the beliefs of the experient or the person interpreting that experience.

The cumulative argument

The cumulative argument is based on the view that if one takes all the different arguments about religious experience together, then they are more convincing than one argument alone. Certainly, if the sheer weight of testimony to religious experience is taken into account, then the debate about whether religious experience is proof of the existence of God would end with a resounding 'yes'. However, weight of testimony is not enough to convince the sceptic, as David Hume's response to the testimony of miracles made clear: 'There is not to be found in all history, any miracle attested by a sufficient number of men, of such unquestioned good sense, education and learning, as to secure us against all delusion' (*An Enquiry Concerning Human Understanding*, 1748).

Furthermore, the principle of cumulative argument is challenged by some on the grounds that several weak arguments put together cannot form one strong argument — rather, they form one large weak argument. The weaknesses of, say, the cosmological argument, are not specifically met by the strengths of the argument from religious experience, and the weaknesses of the argument from religious experience are not cancelled out by the *a priori* claims of the ontological argument.

The principles of testimony and credulity

Richard Swinburne claims that people, in general, tell the truth and that we cannot realistically work on the basis of always doubting their accounts of religious experiences. After all, we do not doubt the basic facts about the world, even though we have not directly experienced them all ourselves. Under his **principle of testimony**, he argues that, unless we have evidence to the contrary, we should believe what people say when they claim to have had a religious experience: 'In the absence of special considerations, the experiences of others are (probably) as they report them'.

Taking it further...

One of the strangest examples of a corporate religious experience occurred just before a major battle in the First World War, when many British soldiers claimed to have seen a vision of the 'Angel of Mons', who protected them from enemy attack.

Swinburne argues that, since people usually tell the truth, there are only three types of evidence that should be taken as rendering their testimonies unreliable, namely:

- if the circumstances surrounding the experience are unreliable, for example through hallucinatory drugs
- if there is particular evidence to suggest that the person is lying
- if the experience can be explained in terms other than God, for example if the person is suffering from a mental illness.

Furthermore, Swinburne suggests that, since so many thousands of people have had an experience of what *seems to them* to be of God, then it is a basic principle of rationality that we should believe them. He called this the **principle of credulity** – that unless we have overwhelming evidence to the contrary, then we should believe that things are as they seem to be. In *The Existence of God* (Oxford University Press, 1979) he wrote: 'How things seem to be is a good guide to how things are…'. Therefore, in his view, religious experiences provide a convincing proof for the existence of God: 'I suggest that the overwhelming testimony of so many millions of people to occasional experiences of God must, in the absence of counter-evidence, be taken as tipping the balance of evidence decisively in favour of the existence of God'.

In support of Swinburne's position, empirical research undertaken in recent years has indicated that as many as 40% of people have, at some time in their lives, had an experience that could be classified as religious.

However, Peter Vardy in *The Puzzle of God* (Fount, 1995) sounds a note of caution. Using the example of someone supposedly seeing a UFO or the Loch Ness monster, he argues that a person, having apparently seen such a phenomenon, could be mistaken and therefore would be right to remain sceptical, unless there were a great deal of evidence to support what he or she had seen: 'The probability of all such experiences must be low, and therefore the quality of the claimed experiences must be proportionately high'.

Arguments against religious experiences as proof for the existence of God

The main difficulty with religious experiences is that they cannot be verified by objective, empirical testing — we cannot carry out a scientific experiment to determine whether they have, in fact, proved the existence of God. Scholars have suggested that they are, at best, ambiguous and can be interpreted in a number of different ways.

Ludwig Wittgenstein used the notion of **seeing-as**, suggesting that, in fact, each person sees their experiences differently; some may think they have experienced God, others may think they have experienced something else. This means that all testimonies concerning religious experiences are unreliable.

Taking it further...

In 1969, the Religious Experience Research Unit in Oxford surveyed people by asking them the question:
Have you at any time in your life had an experience of something completely different from your normal life, whether or not you would describe it as God?
Many responded positively, saying that it was the first time that they had told anyone of their experience, which they said had been one of the most important moments in their lives.

Duck or rabbit? We all see things differently

R. M. Hare talks of religious experiences as a **blik** – that is, an unverifiable and unfalsifiable way of looking at the world. The believer sees or feels something and claims it comes from God. It is their personal interpretation and they believe it to be true. But it cannot be proved true for everyone else and therefore the testimony is unreliable.

Peter Vardy (ibid.) observes:

> The argument from religious experience is, I suggest, going to depend to a very large extent on one's presuppositions. If one's preconceptions favour particular types of experience, one is likely to be convinced by reports of them. If one is a sceptic one will need a great deal of convincing.

John Hick, in *The Existence of God* (Macmillan, 1977), observes that testimonies of religious experiences might also be equally well interpreted in non-religious ways:

> … any special event or experience which can be constituted as manifesting the divine can also be constituted in other ways, and accordingly cannot carry the weight of proof of God's existence.

This is because people cannot experience God in the way they experience either the world or other people, as Peter Cole in *Religious Experience* (Hodder, 2005) points out:

> God is not material, nor does He have a definite location… Can God be recognised?… God is said to be the Creator. How would you recognise that attribute?'

Other critics have suggested that religious experiences could have a natural explanation. For example, they could be brought on by drugs or alcohol or they could be, as Sigmund Freud suggested, a psychological reaction to the hostile world – we feel helpless and so create God in our minds as a great father and protector.

Moreover, there is the issue of consistency. There are many types of religious experience, all vastly different. Yet surely, if God is the source of all of them, there would be greater similarity between them? Why, for instance, don't Hindus see the Virgin Mary or Roman Catholics see Vishnu?

Revelatory experiences are regarded as particularly untrustworthy. In Buddhism, a revelatory experience is not accepted unless the experient is already at a very advanced stage of meditation and unless other high-ranking meditators have shared the insights. Similarly, in the Catholic Church alleged revelations are strictly tested to ensure that they are in line with the teachings of the Church and that the experient is spiritually sound. As Peter Cole observes: 'Only after thirteen years of examination by a commission comprised of clergy, physicians and scientists did the Catholic Church pronounce the Fatima apparitions as worthy of belief… some would still question their authenticity.' Cole goes on to point out that many within Christianity are uneasy about the claims of the Charismatic Movement regarding certain types of religious experience, particularly the phenomenon

Taking it further...

John Hick observes: 'All conscious experience involves recognitions which go beyond what is given to the senses and is thus a matter of experiencing as…' (*The Existence of God*, Macmillan, 1977).

Taking it further...

J. L. Mackie in *The Miracle of Theism* (Oxford, 1992) claims that: 'Religious experience is… essentially incapable of supporting any argument for the traditional central doctrines of theism'.

Taking it further...

The evidence concerning near-death experiences is far from certain and does not, in any event, apply in every case. Scientific opinion remains divided and research published in the highly respected medical journal *The Lancet* in 2001 concludes: 'Our research shows that medical factors cannot account for the occurrence of near-death experience'.

of 'speaking in tongues'. He argues that the experience can be regarded as potentially unreliable and theologically unsound: '... what we see being exhibited today is not the same as speaking in tongues in the New Testament, and natural explanations can explain today's phenomenon'.

Regarding near-death experiences, critics argue that, far from being religious experiences, these are, in fact, some kind of mental phenomenon, possibly caused by a lack of oxygen to the brain, particularly the temporal lobe, which is the centre of emotion.

Summary

In summary, the main arguments against the validity of religious experiences are:

- If God does not exist, there can be no experience of him.

- Any religious experience may be open to a non-religious interpretation.

- Experiences can be deceptive and there are no agreed tests for verifying that an experience comes from God.

- The testimony of religious believers is unreliable, as their views may be affected by their pre-existing religious belief.

- Religious experiences may be the manifestation of psychological needs, for instance to help us to cope with fear of death.

- The emotions and sensations that come with a religious experience can be explained by biological or neurological imbalances in the body.

Richard Dawkins in *The God Delusion* argues: 'If we are gullible, we don't recognise hallucinations or lucid dreaming for what it is and we claim to have seen or heard a ghost; or an angel; or God... such visions and manifestations are certainly not good grounds for believing that ghosts or angels, gods or virgins are actually there'.

On the other hand, Douglas Steere argues that 'As long as it flourishes, it constitutes a continual challenge to what William James calls "a premature closing of accounts with reality" ... The mystic's witness to the accessibility of the living presence...in the hearts of contemporary men and women has been an enormous encouragement to the religious yearnings of men' (Douglas V. Steere, cited in Halverson, M. and Cohen, A. (eds), *A Handbook of Christian Theology*, Fontana, 1960).

Is it meaningful to talk about religious experiences?

To ask whether it is meaningful to speak of religious experiences is to question whether the language of religious experience serves to convey anything of any significance. For the **Logical Positivists** (see page 61), the language of religious experience, as all religious language, was essentially meaningless, since there could be no observations that would serve to verify its claims. Writing in *Language, Truth and Logic* in 1936, A. J. Ayer dismissed the claims to religious experience on the grounds that, although the fact that 'people have religious experiences is interesting from the psychological point of view, it does not in any way imply that there is such a thing as religious knowledge…' (Pelican, 1936). Ayer's position was that if someone claims to have seen God, they tend to make the claim as if it were along the same lines as having claimed to have seen a yellow patch. However, whilst 'the sentence "There exists here a yellow-coloured material thing" expresses a genuine synthetic proposition which could be empirically verified, the sentence "There exists a transcendent god" has no literal significance.' Ayer was criticising the religious experient who moves from asserting that they are experiencing a particular religious emotion to asserting that there exists a transcendent being who is the object of that emotion.

Whilst it is true that, if God does not exist there can be no experience of him, this nevertheless requires proof that there is no God and such clear-cut evidence does not exist. Indeed, theists would argue that the existence of God is a better explanation for many phenomena than science offers. As Richard Swinburne observes: 'In so far as other evidence is ambiguous or counts against but not strongly against the existence of God, our experience (our own or that of many others) ought to tip the balance in favour of God'.

Moreover, although it may be possible for experiences to be open to both religious and non-religious interpretations, it is illogical to assume that all religious interpretations are incorrect. If it is possible to have an experience of God, then it is reasonable to assume that at least some alleged experiences of God actually are experiences of him. It can also be argued that one key empirical test for the validity of a religious experience is to examine the effects that it has on the person who had the experience – how their lives, emotions and feelings have been affected. If they are compatible with what we feel should be expected as a result of experiencing a benevolent divine being, then we may have stronger grounds on which to believe the claim.

Furthermore, there are no grounds for suggesting that the testimonies of religious believers are unreliable. On the contrary, it might be said that religious believers are more able to testify to the validity of a religious experience than a non-believer because they know what to expect. Whilst it is possible that some religious experiences are a manifestation of psychological need, it does not follow that all religious experiences can be explained in this way. If God is, indeed, loving and personal, then, in a sense, we can expect experiences of God to meet our psychological and emotional needs. As Richard Swinburne suggests, God '… will love each of us as individual creatures, and so has reason to intervene… simply to show himself to individuals, and to tell them things individual to themselves'.

Anthony Flew, however, argues that the testimony of religious believers is biased, irrational and questionable and cannot be regarded as meaningful because there is nothing that can count against it. He wrote that religious believers are so convinced of the truth of their religious statements that they often refuse to consider evidence to the contrary. For example, he claims, believers say God is all-loving and all-powerful and they continue to believe this despite the evidence of great suffering in the world, which they choose to ignore: 'What would have to occur or to have occurred to constitute for you a disproof of the love of, or the existence of, God?' (*Theology and Falsification* in *The Existence of God*, ed. Hick, Macmillan, 1977).

Taking it further...

John Hick's principle of **eschatological verification**, and Ward's claim that God may one day verify the religious experiences himself, suggest that verification may finally be realised at the end of time. Hence, religious experiences are weakly verifiable, or verifiable in principle, although they fail the Logical Positivist's test of strong verification.

Taking it further...

Swinburne argues that it is perfectly meaningful for a personal, loving God to make himself known to humanity: 'An omnipotent and perfectly good creator will seek to interact with his creatures and in particular, with human persons capable of knowing him'.

Taking it further...

Flew used John Wisdom's *Parable of the Gardener* to highlight how believers continue to refuse to accept anything that counts against the existence of God. In this story, two men are in an overgrown garden. The first man sees some plants growing among the weeds and suggests that there must be a gardener. But none of the neighbours has ever seen a gardener there. So the first man says that the gardener must come at night. The second man argues that if there was a gardener then he would have removed the weeds. The first man replies that the garden has a design about it, and he suggests that the gardener must be invisible. The men examine the garden and find some things that suggest a gardener, and others that do not. Finally, after both have seen all the evidence, the first insists that there is an invisible gardener, while the other says that there is no gardener at all.

William James

This apparent irrationality among believers is supported by Sam Harris, who wrote in *The End of Faith* (Norton, 2004): 'We have names for people who have many beliefs for which there is no rational justification. When their beliefs are extremely common we call them 'religious', otherwise they are likely to be called 'mad', 'psychotic' or delusional... while religious people are not generally mad, their core beliefs absolutely are'.

Richard Dawkins goes further, claiming that testimonies of religious experiences are simply the manifestation of mental or psychological needs. Religious experiences are an illusion created by the mind to enable people to cope with their fear of the unknown: 'If you've had such an experience, you may find yourself firmly believing that it was real. But don't expect the rest of us to take your word for it, especially if we have the slightest familiarity with the brain and its powerful workings'.

In conclusion, there is no clear-cut answer. Religious experiences are too personal and subjective to provide convincing proof of the existence of God for those who have not had such an experience. However, for those who have, religious experiences are the most convincing proof of all. As William James observed: 'The results of religious experiences are the only reliable basis for judging whether it is a genuine experience of the divine'.

1.2 The ontological argument

Key Ideas

- [ ] Anselm's ontological argument – form and content
- [ ] Strengths and weaknesses of the argument
- [ ] Descartes and the perfect being
- [ ] Challenges to the argument
- [ ] Evaluating the argument

Despite strong attacks over the years from Aquinas, Hume and Kant, and in more recent years from Bertrand Russell, the ontological argument has continued to be popular and to present a strong case for providing grounds for proving the existence of God by use of reason alone. Modern versions from Plantinga and Malcolm have continued to revive it and it serves to raise profound questions about the nature of God, about the relationship between faith and reason and about the nature of philosophical investigations.

The argument fundamentally rests on the premise that there is a universe, but that its existence is contingent – it depends on something else to exist. Whatever provides the explanation for the universe cannot be contingent itself, but is necessary. The ontological argument provides a necessary explanation located in the existence of a supremely perfect being. It argues deductively, not inductively, thus holding out the hope of a universal proof not dependent on empirical evidence about which we may be mistaken.

The form of the ontological argument

Unlike the cosmological and teleological arguments, the ontological (meaning 'concerned with being') argument is *a priori*. This means that the argument does not rely on the evidence of the senses, or the world around us, for either its premises or its conclusion, but rather it moves by stages of logical argument to a conclusion which is **self-evidently true** or **logically necessary**. The argument is also **deductive** and **analytic**. The premises of a deductive argument contain the conclusion that it reaches, and the argument is structured in such a way as to make the conclusion the only possible one that can be deduced from its premises. Because it is analytic, it is true by definition alone. Hence, the argument reaches conclusions about the existence of God that are based on the definition of God used in the premises. Its scope is therefore greater than that of the other arguments for God's existence since they give only a limited view of what God is like, while the concept of God as the most perfect being implies a whole range of qualities.

Taking it further...

Analytic claims are true by definition, hence we do not need any other information to understand what they mean. For example, to say 'Rupert is a bachelor' tells us that Rupert is male and unmarried, since a bachelor is an unmarried male. However, it does not tell us anything else about him – his age, job, appearance, whether he is happy or unhappy – since for that we would need empirical data.

Taking it further...

The argument belongs to **rationalism** in its method of demonstration. It is therefore possible to review the ontological argument without having to become involved in some of the generalisations that haunt discussion of empirical arguments for the existence of God. It is not dependent on accepting or rejecting the views of natural theology or creationism, or on debating the nature of experience.

Saint Anselm (1033–1109)

Taking it further...

The tension in Anselm's thinking lies between the limitations of human reason and his faith. He always strived to find peace in discovering a 'truth so large and deep that it cannot be exhausted by mortals'.

The ontological argument was developed in the period of Christian monastic culture in which grammar, logic and rhetoric were adapted to meet the needs of interpreting scripture and developing systematic theology. In 1078 Anselm, then Archbishop of Canterbury, wrote about matters relating to the Christian faith in the tradition of 'faith seeking understanding', stating that he was 'one who strives to lift his mind to the contemplation of God, and who seeks to understand what he believes'. However, Anselm's striving included the use of proof, a term which is ambiguous – although Anselm believed it was necessary for one who had faith in God as 'that than which nothing greater can be conceived'.

The origins of the argument

Anselm prayed for a single, short argument which would prove almost everything about God, including his nature and existence. As a result, 'Suddenly one night during matins the grace of God illuminated his heart, the whole matter became clear to his mind, and a great joy and exultation filled his inmost being' (The **Proslogion**). The ontological proof was born. For Anselm, the existence of God, held by him to be true by virtue of faith, was now also true by **logical necessity**, relying only on the analysis and meaning of terms and avoiding deduction about the nature of God drawn from the observation of the natural world. The Proslogion offers a form of deductive metaphysics, setting out from self-evident principles in order to answer the central question of metaphysics: *Why should there be any thing at all?* The notion of whether something should 'be' or not focuses the argument very clearly on the problems of what it actually means to say that something exists or has being.

The process of Anselm's reasoning led him to the conclusion that 'Thanks be to thee good Lord, thanks be to thee, because I now understand by thy light what I formerly believed by thy gift'. Effectively, Anselm was trying to prove the existence of God by means of *reductio ad absurdum*. This method of reasoning aims to demonstrate the truth of something by reducing to absurdity the very opposite of what you are aiming to prove. In Anselm's case, the opposite of his conclusion would be that God does not exist, which he aimed to show to be absurd by means of an argument demonstrating that the existence of God is logically necessary (i.e. he cannot *not* exist).

When Anselm argued that the proposition 'God does not exist' is a contradiction as his non-existence is impossible, it demonstrated that philosophy and theology were effectively one and the same process for him. Today, we are used to separating the two disciplines but Anselm, and later Descartes, worked in a time in which it was perfectly reasonable to make the assumption that human reasoning is correct because humans are made in God's image.

It is ironic that Anselm's argument was rejected by other Christian theologians on the grounds that the human intellect is too weak to know enough of God's essence and nature to be able, as Anselm attempted, to deduce from it his necessary existence. Nevertheless, the ontological argument offers one of the most profound issues in philosophy. As Bertrand Russell observed: 'Is there anything we can think of which, by the mere fact that we can think of it, is shown to exist outside our thought?' (*History of Western Philosophy*, Routledge, 2004).

The content of the argument

The argument can be broken down into three stages:

1 The definition of God as 'that than which nothing greater can be conceived' and the implications of this

2 Why the non-existence of God is logically impossible

3 Why 'the fool' believes that which is impossible to be true.

Defining God

Anselm's argument is based on the very word 'God' and what is meant when the word is used. He makes an assumption which is crucial for the argument to work, which is that 'God' is effectively shorthand for 'that than which nothing greater can be conceived' or 'the being than which nothing greater can be thought'. His argument is that when the believer (and the non-believer for that matter) speaks of God, they intuitively understand what is meant by the concept of God – that he is 'greater' than all other beings – not spatially, of course, but in the sense that he is supremely perfect. 'That than which nothing greater can be conceived' *must* possess all perfections in order to be so described and when we speak of God we speak of such a being.

Perfection and existence

Furthermore, Anselm argues that if such a being does indeed possess all perfections, then he must exist. This apparently radical assumption is based on the principle that existence itself is perfection. Anselm places existence into the same category as he would place goodness, love, wisdom or justice, for example, and by so doing he treats it as a defining characteristic.

This step is important to the argument because it establishes that existence may be possessed or lacked, and that to possess existence is necessarily greater than to lack it. Existence may be *in re* (in reality) or merely *in intellectu* (in the mind). That which exists in the mind may hypothetically possess all other great-making qualities, but that which exists in reality is undeniably greater. Anselm writes:

> Now we believe that thou are a being than which none greater can be thought ... clearly that than which a greater cannot be thought cannot exist in the understanding alone. For if it is actually in the understanding alone, it can be thought of as existing in reality, and this is greater. Therefore, if that than which a greater cannot be thought is in the understanding alone, it can be thought of as existing also in reality, and this is greater ... Without doubt, therefore, there exists, both in the understanding and in reality, something than which a greater cannot be thought.

Anselm attempts to clarify his thinking by use of an analogy. When a painter is considering his next work, it is already in his mind and he has a clear idea of it. However, it cannot be said to exist until he has executed it, so that it exists in reality and not just in the mind. Such existence, Anselm maintains, is undeniably greater than existence *in intellectu,* and since God *is* that than

Taking it further...

Obviously, when Anselm speaks of God in these terms, he is not suggesting that God is spatially greater than anything else but rather, that he is the most perfect being conceivable. Note that it is greater to be the most perfect being conceivable than the most perfect being that exists, although for God to be 'that than which nothing greater can be conceived', he must exist in reality, not just as a concept.

Taking it further...

Consider whether existing in reality is a greater perfection than existing in the mind. There are things the non-existence of which we would consider to be more perfect than their existence – for example cancer, evil dictators or tsunamis. Furthermore, some things which exist in the mind are more perfect than those which exist in reality – the perfect partner in the mind is unlikely to be matched detail for detail in reality, and yet we would presumably prefer the imperfect partner *in re* than the perfect partner who exists only *in intellectu.*

which nothing greater can be conceived, God must possess the perfection of existence both in reality and in the mind. If this was not the case, then something other than God that did exist in reality would be greater than God, and this is impossible.

Thinking through the argument

Like all the arguments for the existence of God, the ontological argument can be set out in various series of premises and a conclusion. This helps our understanding of how its logic appears to work. Consider these examples:

1 God exists *or* does not exist.
2 If God *does not* exist, then a greater being can be conceived, but this is impossible (a *reductio ad absurdum*).
3 Therefore, to say God *does not* exist is a logical impossibility.
4 Therefore, God exists.

---

1 God exists either in the understanding alone *or* in the understanding and in reality.
2 That which exists in reality is greater than that which exists in the understanding alone.
3 God is that than which nothing greater can be conceived.
4 If God is that than which nothing greater can be conceived, then he must possess all perfections, including real existence.
5 If God did not possess real existence, something else, which did possess real existence, would be greater than God.
6 This is a logical impossibility, given the definition of God (**3**).
7 Therefore, God exists in reality.

---

1 God is that than which none greater can be thought.
2 The concept of God exists in the understanding.
3 God is a possible being (i.e. he may exist in reality).
4 If God *only* exists in the mind and is *only* a possible being, he could have been greater than he actually is – if he also existed in reality.
5 If this is so, then God is a being than which a greater *can* be thought.
6 This is impossible, for God is a being than which *none* greater can be thought.
7 Therefore, God exists in reality as well as in the mind.

The concept of necessary existence

In all this, Anselm makes clear that his understanding of God is of a being possessing **necessary existence**. This concept was integral to the cosmological argument too, but it applies differently to the ontological argument. In this case, God's necessary existence is *de dicto* necessary – by definition. Because the definition of God requires that he should exist, to deny his existence would be absurd. When this is fully understood, it is impossible to deny the existence of God, as Anselm explains:

> *For something can be thought of as existing which cannot be thought of as not existing, and this is greater than that which can be thought of as not existing ... So, then, there truly is a being than which a greater cannot be thought – so truly that it cannot even be thought of as not existing ... He therefore who understands that God thus exists cannot think of him as non-existent.*

Taking it further...

Try thinking of this part of the argument in terms of something that we know exists – elephants, for example – and something that we know does not exist – say, unicorns. Unicorns exist *in intellectu*, but although we may have a clear idea of what they entail, their existence is limited to the mind. Elephants exist both *in intellectu* (we have the idea of the elephant in the mind) and *in re* (we can locate them in time and space). Elephants are therefore greater than unicorns.

Taking it further...

In Thomas Aquinas's third way, he reasoned that God's existence was necessary in order for the contingent world to exist at all. In this way, he argued for God's necessary existence *de re*, by the very nature of things. Anselm's argument is quite different, in that conclusions drawn about the nature of the world are irrelevant to questions of God's existence; rather, the necessary existence of God is established by simply evaluating what it means to speak of God at all.

The fool believes the impossible to be true

Anselm is, of course, aware that the existence of God can, and is, denied by the atheist. In response to this, he cites Psalm 53 – 'the fool has said in his heart there is no God.' The Psalmist's fool is the atheist who, Anselm observes, says what is impossible to say since it cannot possibly be true: that God does not exist. Nevertheless, the atheist does say this and Anselm explains that this is because the atheist has failed to understand the full implications of the concept of God. Had the atheist grasped the real meaning of God as that than which nothing greater can be conceived, it would be impossible for him to deny his existence. In order to deny the existence of God, the atheist must at least have a concept of God in his understanding. It is then only a short step to recognising the impossibility of denying the existence of such a being:

> Can it be that there is no such being, since the fool hath said in his heart 'There is no God' ... But when this same fool hears what I am saying – 'A being than which none greater can be thought' – he understands what he hears ... even if he does not understand that it exists ... Even the fool, then, must be convinced that a being than which none greater can be thought exists at least in his understanding.

Throughout the **Proslogion**, Anselm returns to what Descartes was later concerned to investigate – the quest for intelligibility, reaching beyond mere words to articulate his proof for God's existence. He was aware that words can be ambiguous and misleading, but from this perspective, his arguments were an analytical commentary on the concept of the God of Classical Theism rather than a proof of his existence as such. Anselm deduces the attributes of God from the perfection that is inherent in the concept of God itself.

Taking it further...

Needless to say, for the atheist, this argument is futile, since the fact that atheism can be held as a rationally consistent position (i.e. it is equally possible to experience the world consistently as an atheist or as a theist) means that the non-existence of God can be conceived as rationally certain.

Strengths and weaknesses of the argument

What are the strengths of Anselm's position?

- **It holds out the hope of a proof.**
  It is a deductive argument. If valid, it will be proof for both believer and atheist.

- **Its starting point is valid for both believer and atheist.**
  The definition of God as 'that than which nothing greater can be conceived' is accepted by the atheist, even if the atheist denies that such a being exists. The atheist must have an understanding of God in order to be able to reject belief in God.

- **It is an intellectually stimulating argument that continues to be studied and debated.**
  It is reasonable to assume, therefore, that there are good reasons to consider the argument, in some way, to be sound.

Where does Anselm fail?

The idea of God as 'that than which nothing greater can be conceived' is:

- **not coherent**
  How can God be omniscient? He cannot know human future choices.

- **mutually inconsistent**
  No being could be both omniscient and omnipotent, since an omnipotent being could make a creature who had a secret unknown to anyone but itself, while an omniscient being must know every secret.

- **leading to a useless God**
  Even supposing we can make sense of the great-making properties and show them to be mutually consistent, won't the concept of God that we arrive at be so distant from religious experience as to be useless?

- **assumed by Anselm to be beyond criticism**
  However, it cannot be assumed that this is the only logical way of defining God. For the process theologians, for example, a better definition of God is as 'the fellow sufferer who understands'. Other believers may also be satisfied with a definition of God which permits him to be understood as less than supremely perfect, without unacceptably destroying or qualifying his nature. However, it may be reasonable to say that, whatever a person believes about God, nothing can be thought to be greater than God.

Substantiating the concept of God and showing that there really is something to which the concept of God refers, are two quite different processes and the first does not lead to the second. Definitions only tell us what God would be like if he existed. It cannot establish whether he does in fact exist. One can move from a concept of imagination to a concept of reality, but not from a concept of imagination to reality. Hence there is no contradiction in denying the reality of a conceptual being that has all perfections. When we say that existence is part of God's definition, we are merely saying that no non-existing being can be God.

Descartes and the perfect being

Five hundred years after Anselm, the influential French thinker René Descartes (1598-1650) reformulated the ontological proof, in terms of the concept of necessary existence. He believed that, in proving the existence of God, he would proceed by unaided human reason, discounting the evidence of the senses. It appealed to him as a rationalist philosopher to seek to prove the existence of God by reason alone, rejecting as untrustworthy information that comes from the senses alone. Doubting all his knowledge, he realised that the very act of doubting proved his own existence, inspiring the famous saying *Cogito, ergo sum* (I think, therefore I am). Like Anselm, Descartes wanted believers to realise that, when they use the world 'God', they mean an infinitely perfect being superior to all beings in perfection. He maintained that the use of reason enabled the terms to be clarified in a distinct and intelligible way.

As Descartes could conceive of his own existence, he could also conceive of the existence of a perfect being:

1 I exist.
2 In my mind, I have the concept of a perfect being.
3 As an imperfect being, I could not have conjured up the concept of a perfect being.
4 The concept of a perfect being must therefore have originated from the perfect being itself.
5 A perfect being must exist in order to be perfect.
6 Therefore, a perfect being exists.

or:

René Descartes

Taking it further...

It can be said that Anselm's argument is not a valid deductive argument because:

- Existence is not a great-making property. The word 'exist' merely states that a concept has an actuality.
- Existence can never be an analytic proposition. Propositions about existence are not analytic but are synthetic and contingent.
- It is impossible to define things into existence.

1 The idea of God is the idea of a supremely perfect being.
2 A supremely perfect being has all perfections.
3 Existence is a perfection.
4 A supremely perfect being has the perfection of existence.
5 It is impossible to think of God as not existing.
6 Therefore, God exists.

Descartes maintained existence belonged analytically to God in the same way that three angles are analytically predicated of a triangle, or, less convincingly, as a valley is a necessary predicate of a mountain. However, whilst we may agree – both that our own existence is something of which we can be certain, and that the necessary essence of a triangle is triangularity – Descartes may have a notion of a perfect being, but this is not to say that everyone shares that notion. Descartes suggested that the notion of a perfect being is in some way innate, but this seems to be something of a simplification. He also claimed that an imperfect being cannot think up the concept of a perfect being. We can surely conceive of as many perfect things, people or beings as we please and, allowing for the fact that no two people are likely to share exactly the same concept of what constitutes a perfect being, the only question that remains is whether they then therefore exist in reality or not.

Objections to Anselm's proof

Aquinas's objection to Anselm's argument and his method was concerned with both the ambiguity of the terms Anselm used, and also with the intellectual arrogance which he believed underpinned the argument. Although Aquinas acknowledged that God's existence necessarily involves his nature as a perfect being, he rejected the assumption of the proof that fallible human intellect alone can prove the existence of God. Weak human reason *can* conceive of God not existing and, Aquinas suggested, only God could understand the ontological proof!

Aquinas questioned another important aspect of the ontological argument, claiming that Anselm was guilty of making a 'transitional error' – that is, moving from the definition of God to the existence of God. Furthermore, Aquinas observed that Anselm was guilty of making an assumption about the definition of God that was not necessarily shared by all believers. Understanding the meaning of the term 'God' means only that God exists in the understanding, not in reality. God's existence in reality must be demonstrated *a posteriori*, as Aquinas's cosmological argument attempts to show. Kant similarly maintained that empirical data is the only reliable way of knowing anything about the universe and that hence a move from definition to reality is a false manoeuvre.

Despite these criticisms, the strength of Anselm's argument is that he insists on God as a being who is without limits and non-contingent. His greatness and perfection is such that he is free from the contingencies which characterise all other beings and therefore, since he differs from humans in this respect, his non-existence is not logically possible. Hence, we return to the subtle but important point that God's existence is, by definition, not open to any kind of empirical proof; thus, being beyond such a proof is proof of his existence!

Taking it further...

Aquinas's rejection of the argument is consistent with modern philosophy's rejection of the proof, on the grounds that it showed the 'abuse of human rational faculties' (Stephen Mulhall, *Faith and Reason*, Duckworth, 1998).

Gaunilo and the perfect island

Anselm's argument was refuted in his own lifetime by Gaunilo, who demonstrated in a *reductio ad absurdum* of his own that, if the logic of the argument were applied to things other than God, it led to invalid conclusions: 'This being is said to be in my understanding already, only because I understand what is said. Now could it not with equal justice be said that I have in my understanding all manner of unreal objects, having absolutely no existence in themselves, because I understand these things if one speaks of them, whatever they may be?' (*On Behalf of the Fool*)

Replacing the word 'God' with 'the greatest island' led to an argument which had the same *form* as Anselm's, with true premises, and yet which leads to a false conclusion:

1 I can conceive of an island that than which no greater island can be thought.
2 Such an island must possess all perfections.
3 Existence is a perfection.
4 Therefore, the island exists.

We can all conceive of a perfect island

Even if 'the greatest island' were substituted for 'the greatest *possible* island' the argument would still lead to an invalid conclusion, since quite clearly to conceive of an island in all of its perfections does not guarantee its existence or bring it into existence.

However, Gaunilo's criticism was exposed by Anselm as revealing a misunderstanding of the argument's purpose. Anselm observed that his proof was intended only to apply to necessary beings, not to contingent beings or items, such as an island, which may or may not exist. Furthermore, there is no logical point at which we might reasonably say that we have reached intrinsic perfection in an island or other contingent item. There is always something more which can be added to make it more perfect, and our concept of perfection in islands, or other contingent things, is surely subjective – I cannot possible guarantee that my perfect island is the same as yours.

Kant: Existence is not a predicate

Fundamental to both Anselm's and Descartes' form of the ontological argument is that existence is a **predicate** – an attribute or quality that can be possessed or lacked, such as size, shape, colour, temperature, personality traits or intelligence. These may or may not belong to a thing or being, and their presence or absence is part of our understanding and apprehension of it. However, Kant observed that existence is not associated with the definition of something, since it does not add to our understanding of that thing. We must establish the existence of something before we can say what it is like, not the other way around, and so if there is a perfect being then he must exist, just as if there is a triangle, it must have three sides, but we cannot ascribe existence *a priori* to our definition of a perfect being. That is tantamount to saying 'An existing God exists'.

'It would be self-contradictory to posit a triangle and yet reject its three angles, but there is no contradiction in rejecting the triangle together with its three angles' (*Critique of Pure Reason*, ed. 1965, St Masturus Press).

Taking it further...

Kant's position was that existence added nothing to the concept of a thing or being. For example, £100 in the imagination was not made greater in number or nature by existing in reality. However, arguably, £100 in reality is substantially more useful than £100 in the mind since it has practical value. In the same way, God who exists only in the mind can have no real effect on the lives of believers. God who exists in reality can intervene in people's lives and make a real difference.

Douglas Gasking: The ontological proof for the non-existence of God

The Australian philosopher, Douglas Gasking, also offered *reductio* to demonstrate the fallacy of the ontological proof.

1 The creation of the world is the most supreme achievement conceivable.
2 The value of an achievement is measured by its intrinsic quality *and* the ability of its creator.
3 The greater the limitation of the creator, the more impressive the achievement.
4 The greatest limitation of a creator would be non-existence.
5 Therefore, a world created by a non-existent creator would be greater than one created by an existent creator.
6 An existing God is therefore not the greatest conceivable being, since an even greater being would be one which did not exist.

Conclusion: God does not exist.

Obviously, this does not *prove* the non-existence of God but, in the same way, Anselm's argument does not prove that he does exist, either.

Evaluating the argument

Support for Kant

The 20th-century philosopher, G. E. Moore, demonstrated further the strength of Kant's principle that existence could not be grammatically used as a predicate because the word does not function as other predicates. He proposed taking the following statements:

A Some tame tigers do not growl.
B Some tame tigers do not exist.

Statement A is perfectly meaningful, implying that there are such beings that answer to the description 'tame tiger' and that a characteristic of some of them is that they do not growl. However, statement B, which uses 'do not exist' in the same way as 'do not growl' was used in statement A, is not meaningful in the same way. We learn nothing about tame tigers in this statement apart from the fact that they do not exist, which presumably means there is nothing to learn about them anyway!

Bertrand Russell also took Kant's observations further. He proposed that 'existence' was not a predicate but rather a term used to indicate the instance of something in the spatio-temporal world. Therefore, 'Some tame tigers exist' does not tell us anything about their nature but it does indicate that there is an instance of such beings in the world. 'Cows are brown' and 'Cows are brown and exist' effectively tell us only one thing: 'Cows are brown'. 'And exist' indicates that they occupy a place in the world, but it is a tautology since by saying that they are brown we are presumably referring to existent cows rather than imaginary ones in any case.

Taking it further...

Russell proposed that the two claims 'Cows exist' and 'Unicorns do not exist' do not say that they have or do not have a particular attribute of existence. Rather, we use them to say that one has an instance (cows) and one does not (unicorns).

Taking it further...

Interestingly, Russell had, as a young man, been almost convinced that the argument worked: 'I remember the precise moment, one day in 1894, as I was walking along Trinity Lane, when I saw in a flash (or thought I saw) that the ontological argument is valid. I had gone out to buy a tin of tobacco; on the way back, I suddenly threw it up in the air, and exclaimed as I caught it: 'Great Scott, the ontological argument is sound' (*The God Delusion*, Bantam Press, 2006).

Taking it further...

'Both Hume and Kant showed that it is not possible to move from the *de dicto* necessity of a proposition to the *de re* necessity of God ... They also challenged the very idea of anything being necessary, maintaining that the only things that are necessary are linguistic statements where truth represents convention (for instance, *de dicto* necessary statements such as 'all triangles have three angles')' (Peter Vardy, *What is Truth?*, University of New South Wales Press, 1999).

Nevertheless, it is important that we distinguish between claims about existence which *appear* to function in the same way because they are grammatically the same. For example, consider these two claims:

> **A** All cows have tails.
> **B** All unicorns have horns.

Grammatically, these claims are identical, and it is therefore reasonable to assume, according to Russell's reasoning, that cows and unicorns occupy time and space. However, whilst it would correspond to facts about the real world to say 'All cows have tails [and exist]', it would not be true in the same way to say 'All unicorns have horns [and exist]'. Hence, the logical structure of a claim is not enough to provide implicit information about the existence of its subject. Rather, we need some other information about a thing or being in order to make accurate claims about its existence.

David Hume

David Hume considered the argument a failure because it made a false assumption about existence – that necessary existence was a coherent concept. He argued that existence could only ever be contingent (dependent and limited) and that all statements about existence could be denied without contradiction. All things which could be said to exist could also be said not to exist. Hume argued in *Dialogues Concerning Natural Religion*: 'However much our concept of an object may contain, we must go outside of it to determine whether or not it exists. We cannot define something into existence – even if it has all the perfections we can imagine'.

Support for the argument

Despite the work of these influential critics, the argument has also been supported by leading thinkers. Amongst them is **Leibniz**, who argued that since it is impossible to think of God as lacking any perfection – 'a simple quality which is positive and absolute, and expresses without limitation whatever it does' – he must exist, since to possess all perfections but not to exist, would be meaningless. Recent formulations of the argument have maintained that God's necessary existence is existence which cannot be brought about or be threatened by anything else.

Norman Malcolm proposed another form of the argument in support of necessary existence, based on the presumption that if God *could* exist, he *does* exist, since he cannot not exist. The argument can be framed thus:

> 1 God is that than which nothing greater can be thought.
> 2 Necessary existence is a perfection.
> 3 If God possesses all perfections, he must possess necessary existence.
> 4 A necessary being cannot not exist.
> 5 If God *could* exist then he would exist necessarily.
> 6 It is contradictory to say that a necessary being does not exist.
> 7 Therefore, God must exist.

Furthermore, Malcolm argued that God's existence is either necessary or impossible, but that he cannot possess contingent existence. Hence, God must have necessary existence. Malcolm observed that God is a special case, unlike contingent beings that have only possible existence. However, as we have already seen, if we adopt Hume's view, necessary existence may be an incoherent concept and so Malcolm's form of the argument will fail. Furthermore, whilst Malcolm's argument may show that *if* God exists, he exists necessarily, that is not the same as proving that he *does* exist.

Malcolm also questioned whether the notion that existence is a perfection was a reasonable doctrine to pursue: 'The doctrine that existence is a perfection is remarkably queer. It makes sense and is true to say that my future house will be a better one if it is insulated than if it is not insulated, but what could it mean to say that it will be a better house if it exists than if it does not' (cited in Dawkins, ibid., 2006).

Alvin Plantinga suggested that since we are able to imagine any number of alternative worlds in which things may be quite different – for example, a world in which Luciano Pavarotti did not choose to become an operatic tenor, but was a house painter instead – there must be any number of possible worlds, including our own. However, if God's existence is necessary, he must exist in them all and have all the characteristics of God in them all. This is because, Plantinga argued, God is both **maximally great** and **maximally excellent**. He proposed that:

> A There exists a world in which there is a being of maximal greatness.
> B A being of maximal excellence is omnipotent, omniscient and omnibenevolent in all worlds.

Nevertheless, Plantinga's argument only succeeds in showing that God is possible in all possible worlds, not that he is actual in all possible worlds.

Bear in mind, however, that if there is a world of maximal greatness and a being of maximal excellence, there is no reason why there should not also be a being of maximal evil occupying all possible worlds. Plantinga's form of the argument does not therefore prove the exclusiveness of the omnipotent God.

Richard Dawkins

The well-known contemporary atheist, Richard Dawkins, rejects the ontological argument on the grounds, firstly, that it is 'infantile'. He writes:

> *Let me translate this infantile argument into the appropriate language, which is the language of the playground:*
> *'Bet you I can prove God exists.'*
> *'Bet you can't.'*
> *'Right then, imagine the most perfect perfect **perfect** thing possible.'*
> *'Okay, now what?'*
> *'Now, is that perfect perfect **perfect** thing real? Does it exist?'*
> *'No, it's only in my mind.'*
> *'But if it was real it would be even more perfect, because a really really perfect thing would have to be better than a silly old imaginary thing. So I've proved that God exists. Nur Nurny Nur. All atheists are fools.'*

(*The God Delusion*, Bantam Press, 2006)

Taking it further...

Another way of understanding Malcolm's approach is to consider the possible ways of conceiving of God's existence:
- God does not exist.
- God exists contingently.
- God exists necessarily.

We are obliged to reject the first claim, since by definition God's non-existence is inconceivable. We must also reject the second claim since, if God existed contingently, his existence would be no greater than the existence of any other being. Thus, we have no alternative other than to accept that God exists necessarily, since by rejecting the first two claims, we have accepted that he cannot *not* exist.

Taking it further...

This form of the argument is the **modal form**, since the idea of possible worlds is used by philosophers to determine the modality of statements. The three modes are **necessity**, **impossibility** and **possibility**. To test for logical impossibility, we need to think of a possible world in which a statement is true. If it is possible to do so, the statement is not logically impossible.

Dawkins says that the fact the 'grand conclusion' that God exists 'could follow from such logo-machist trickery offends me aesthetically'. He supports Bertrand Russell's claims that 'It is easier to feel convinced that the ontological argument must be fallacious than it is to find out precisely where the fallacy lies'. Dawkins argues that the automatic reaction to the argument should be suspicion that any line of reasoning which lacked a 'single piece of data from the real world' should have lead to such a significant conclusion.

Anti-realism

It can be argued that the ontological argument is successful if we accept that the statements made are not objectively true statements but are subjectively true statements, which, Peter Vardy explains, 'cohere with other true statements made within a particular form of life'. Proponents of the ontological argument are already committed to certain claims, most especially that God is that than which nothing greater can be conceived, and all that this entails. Anselm maintained that the existence of God was necessary and self-evident, and on this assumption the ontological argument cannot fail. However, 'God necessarily exists' is a claim that may be rejected by realists as meaningless, unverifiable and unfalsifiable, because it does not correspond to the state of affairs which it describes. The anti-realist approach does not demand absolute truth, but rather that something should be true within its peculiar context. Hence, for Anselm and his supporters the claim that God is, *de dicto*, necessarily existent, is true within their particular 'form of life', as are other claims made within the religious system to which a believer subscribes.

Language games

However, arguably, modern anti-realist ideas, such as those of Wittgenstein's language games (see page 70), are not always of much value in theology. For example, it is of little use to say that prayer has a practical value in bringing comfort to the worshipper, since for the believer the act of praying assumes that God exists. Norman Malcolm argued that in Psalm 90 God is conceived of as a being to which existence necessarily belongs: 'Before the mountains were brought forth … even from everlasting to everlasting, thou art God'. It is internally consistent to the Psalmist that this is what they mean when they describe God in these terms. In the same way, the ontological proof is a language game, the purpose of which is to explain the nature of a divine being through a method of discourse which is internally coherent to the speaker. It is therefore beside the point whether God does or does not exist. Anselm's argument raised the question of whether the assumption about God's existence can be reconciled with a particular use of language.

Deductive reasoning

The success of the ontological argument also depends on how successfully it works as a deductive proof. Without the evidence and experience of the universe on which to draw, the argument must be analytically sound. In this respect, it may be successful if the first premise is universally accepted. However, whilst 'God is that than which nothing greater can be conceived' may be true for *some* believers, it is not necessarily the case for all. If

Taking it further...

Despite the criticisms outlined by its opponents, the ontological argument could be considered to succeed if it is understood as an expression of what the believer already holds to be true, rather than as proof that an objective reality to which the term 'God' is ascribed, exists objectively in the objective universe.

believers in God can understand other terms or describe him in other ways, or if there are good reasons for rejecting Anselm's definition, then the argument fails. Only if *true* premises lead to valid conclusions can a deductive argument be said to have fully succeeded. This cannot be said of the ontological argument, and as such it is flawed.

Anselm claims in the **Proslogion** that for his proof to work he does not require that God be understood, only that certain terms be understood, and he takes it as read that his proof shows the rational necessity or belief in God. Although it does not achieve this, his proof does show that we cannot reject God's existence as a matter of fact. It is a great achievement of Anselm that the proof demonstrates how human reason, by its very nature, goes beyond what experience warrants. However, reason itself cannot show that an absolutely necessary being exists or does not exist.

What the argument does show is that humans are clearly disposed to speculate about what lies beyond experience and to believe things about the transcendent, and repeated attempts by 20th-century philosophers have failed to eliminate this.

Taking it further...

Kant observed that Hume's principle not to carry the use of reason dogmatically beyond the field of all possible experience needs to be matched by another: 'Not to consider the field of human experience as one which bounds itself in the eyes of our reason' (Sebastian Gardner, *Kant and the Critique of Pure Reason*, Routledge, 1998).

1.3 Atheism and critiques of religious belief

Key Ideas

- **Defining atheism and agnosticism**
- **Sociological critiques of religious belief**
- **Psychological critiques**
- **Popularist critiques**
- **Is theism stronger than atheism?**

Atheism

'Of all choices, atheism requires the greatest faith, as it demands that one's limited store of human knowledge is sufficient to exclude the possibility of God' (Francis Collins of the Human Genome Project).

Atheism means, literally, 'without/no God'. However, there are many reasons *why* people may hold an atheistic position and it should not be assumed that all atheists have reached that position via the same journey. Furthermore, atheism can be either strong or weak. 'Weak atheism' is simple scepticism, the absence of belief in the existence of God. 'Strong atheism' is an explicitly-held belief that God does not exist. Strong atheism is often expressed as **antitheism**. An antitheist offers strong arguments against the religious belief of others, considering them wrong or dangerous, rather than simply choosing not to believe for themselves.

Taking it further...

In *God, Freedom, and Immortality: A Critical Analysis* (Prometheus, 1984), Andrew Flew considers the meaning of the word 'atheist' thus:

The word 'atheism' ... has in this contention to be construed unusually. Whereas nowadays the usual meaning of 'atheist' in English is 'someone who asserts there is no such being as God', I want the word to be understood not positively but negatively. I want the original Greek prefix 'a' to be read in the same way in 'atheist' as it customarily is read in such other Greco-English words as 'amoral', 'atypical', and 'asymmetrical'. In this interpretation an atheist becomes: someone who is simply not a theist. Let us, for future ready reference, introduce the labels 'positive atheist' for the former and 'negative atheist' for the latter.

Taking it further...

'I am an atheist and this means at least: I do not believe there is a god, or any gods, personal or in nature, or manifesting himself, herself, or itself in any way ... There are no supernatural forces, no supernatural entities such as gods, or heavens, or hells, or life or death ... nor can there be' (Madalyn Murray O'Hair, Founder of American Atheists Inc.).

In Western culture, atheists are frequently assumed to have no religious or spiritual beliefs. However, some religious and spiritual beliefs that deny a creator God (forms of Buddhism, for example) have been described as broadly atheistic, whilst Hinduism includes both theistic and atheistic forms. Those who describe themselves as atheists in the modern world tend, in the main, towards secular ideologies such as humanism, rationalism, and naturalism. However, there is no one ideology, set of beliefs or practices that all atheists adhere to, any more than theists do.

Interestingly, it may be possible to describe a person who has no *knowledge* of theistic belief as atheist. This category would therefore include children without the conceptual ability to grasp the issues involved in theism – they do not yet believe in God and so are atheist.

The basis of atheism

An atheist may adopt their position for several reasons, including:

- The view that there is no such being to whom the description 'God' can be given. For example, Logical Positivism held that since 'God' is a metaphysical term, it is meaningless even to ask questions about the existence of God, let alone believe in it. Atheistic claims were considered no more meaningful than theistic claims.

- All apparent experiences of God can be accounted for in other ways. Samuel Butler wrote: 'Theist and atheist – the fight between them is as to whether God shall be called God or have some other name' (cited in *The Pan Dictionary of Religious Quotations*, ed. Margaret Pepper, 1991). So, whilst an atheist may claim that a mystical experience is the result of a feverish hallucination, the theist claims that they are direct experiences of the divine.

- The view that apparently contradictory states of affairs in the world – evil and suffering, for example – count decisively against the existence of God. 'The existence of a world without a God seems to me less absurd than the presence of a God, existing in all his perfections, creating an imperfect man to make him run the risk of Hell' (Armand Salacrou, cited in *The Pan Dictionary of Religious Quotations*).

- The view that believers in God are deluded or have been deluded by religious leaders for their own unscrupulous purposes

- Dislike and distrust of organised religion, which leads to a rejection of belief in God. Religious systems can be satisfactorily explained in terms of social, psychological, or political factors.

- Holding false beliefs about God – for example, that he is powerless, although benevolent – or denying expectations and propositions made in the Bible

- A hatred of religious beliefs and believers. This is 'the sort of atheist who does not so much disbelieve in God as personally dislike him' (George Orwell, cited in *The Pan Dictionary of Religious Quotations*).

- The view that belief in God serves only to support those who are emotionally, intellectually, or psychologically weak

- Loss of faith, unanswered prayer, false teachers and bad experiences of religion

- Contradictory teachings and lack of logical coherence
- Fear of the moral and spiritual accountability which usually accompanies religious belief.

The burden of proof

The factors listed above do not, in themselves, prove anything – they are reasons for non-belief, or for rejection of religious belief, in the same way that theists offer reasons for belief. However, many atheists adopt the position that the burden of proof lies with the theist to prove that, despite the lack of evidence in support of God's existence and the wealth of evidence which appears to count against it, God exists.

However, theists who are confident of their position declare that the onus is on the atheist to demonstrate why it is any easier to argue in favour of the non-existence of God. Either way, as Peter Vardy observes: 'To seek the truth may mean overcoming the fear that one's own certainties and most cherished convictions may be wrong, or the fear of facing the consequences of a claim to truth' (*What is Truth?* University of New South Wales, 1999).

The philosophical problem of atheism versus theism may be set out in several ways, where X represents God:

- If X cannot be proved to exist, then X does not exist.
  This view is a strong empirical position which rejects belief in anything which cannot be empirically demonstrated.

- If X cannot be proved to exist, then X cannot be proved not to exist.
  This position renders both theism and atheism equally unsound from a philosophical perspective.

- If X cannot be proved not to exist, then X must exist.
  If arguments against the existence of God fail, then by default God must exist.

- If X cannot be proved not to exist, then X may exist.
  Failure to disprove the existence of God does not render his existence necessary, but it is probable.

Agnosticism

Agnosticism holds that it is not possible to know whether God exists, or to know his nature. The term was coined in the 19th century by Thomas Huxley, as the opposite of *gnostic*, the Greek term used in the early church to describe those who professed to have special revelatory knowledge of the divine. An agnostic may well claim to be open to the possibility of knowledge leading to belief rather than non-belief, but may not be able to say what it would take for them to do so. Hence, it is possible to say that agnosticism is merely another form of atheism.

Agnosticism is essentially concerned with the problem of what we can genuinely know. The critical philosophy of David Hume brought into question the status and character of positive knowledge. He pointed out that only

> **Taking it further...**
>
> 'When believers are challenged to prove that God exists, it is a standard reaction to insist that the existence of God cannot be disproved. Of course it cannot be disproved; it is impossible to prove a negative; the onus of proof is on the positive. It is up to believers to prove evidence of the objective reality of God' (Derek Chatterton, *Reflections on Religion*, pub. D Chatterton, 1998).

Taking it further...

'Positively, the principle may be expressed: In matters of the intellect, follow your reason as far as it will take you, without regard to any other consideration. And negatively: In matters of the intellect, do not pretend that conclusions are certain which are not demonstrated or demonstrable. That I take to be the agnostic faith, which if a man keep whole and undefiled, he shall not be ashamed to look the universe in the face, whatever the future may have in store for him' (T. H. Huxley, *Agnosticism*, 1889).

Taking it further...

'It was because he was convinced about the social utility of religion and of religious concord that Napoleon made up his mind to restore the unity and prosperity of the Church.' (Alec Vidler, *The Pelican History of the Church*)

knowledge of regular, observable sequences and connections could constitute positive knowledge; it did not imply knowledge of causes, powers, natures, essences or purposes. This began the disassociation of science from metaphysics. With the steady progress of the sciences and the analytical attention paid by philosophers to what scientists were doing, it became abundantly clear that science was capable of dealing only with questions that arose in the course of research that could be tested. Loose questions, general questions, questions about causes and origins, and other traditional metaphysical questions, were not the kind with which science was, or ever would be, competent to deal. By the time Huxley invented the word 'agnosticism', the onus was on the believer to justify his belief, to show why he should be taken seriously.

Critiques of religious belief

Critiques of religious belief analyse the role and function of religion in society or in the lives of individuals, invariably drawing the conclusion that, independently of God's existence, religion creates social and hierarchical structures which have a powerful effect on the lives of individuals and communities. Typically, a critique of religious belief will reach the conclusion that 'God' is the name given to something else – for example, society, or political leaders – and that in turn religious beliefs and practices are functionally or projectively explained. A functional explanation of religion identifies the **function** it serves in society, which may, on examination, ultimately have nothing to do with the existence and worship of God, who exists objectively in the world. A projective explanation identifies the way in which humans **project** their fears, anxieties and subconscious feelings on to the object of worship. The existence of religion serves to maintain a social structure of benefit to some, but not others, and prevents the individual from realising the full potential of their humanity. In some cases, the critique may go as far as to say that religious beliefs serve to deceive the individual or the group as to what is truly real.

Sociological critiques

Sociologists may perceive religion as more than belief in God or the supernatural, but as a system which attempts an ultimate solution to explaining human existence or which serves a function within society as a whole.

Emile Durkheim

Emile Durkheim's functionalist theory of religion argues that religion serves to unite and preserve the community. He defined religion as: 'A unified system of beliefs and practices relative to sacred things... beliefs and practices which unite into one single moral community called a church, all who adhere to them' (*The Elementary Forms of Religious Life,* The Free Press, 1954). Durkheim saw religion as one of the forces that create within individuals a sense of moral obligation to adhere to society's demands. He was not concerned with the variety of religious experience of individuals but rather with the communal activity and the communal bonds to which participation in religious activities lead, and was concerned to examine the mechanisms that might serve to shore up a threatened social order. In this respect he was in quest of what would today be described as functional equivalents for religion in a fundamentally non-religious or a-religious age.

Durkheim likened a religious community to a primitive clan that worshipped a totem, symbolising God and the unity of the clan. The clan and God are one and the same, hence there is no separate entity called God, and thus God does not exist simply by virtue of religious belief and practice. What does exist is a unified social system which believes that it owes its being to God. This belief is expressed in shared rituals, values and identity; it discourages change, and explains phenomena that otherwise make little sense. Religion, he argued, is not only a social creation, but is in fact society divinised – it is effectively made into the divine object of worship. Durkheim stated that the deities which men worship together are only projections of the power of society. Religion is essentially social, occurring in a social context, and when men celebrate sacred things, they unwittingly celebrate the power of the society to which they give sacred significance. He went on to argue that modern man needed to recognise that he had become dependent on the society to which he had given religious significance, and must 'discover the rational substitutes for these religious notions that for a long time have served as the vehicle for the most essential moral ideas' (*Moral Education*, The Free Press, 1961).

Durkheim was keen to urge people to unite in a civic morality based on the recognition that we are what we are because of society. Society acts within us to elevate us, not unlike the way in which the divine spark was said to transform ordinary humans into creatures capable of transcending their physical, intellectual and emotional capacity.

Criticisms of Durkheim's view

- Religious believers distinguish between membership of their religious community and belief in God. Although membership of the religious community is important, their primary loyalty is to God not to the community.

- The theory does not explain how religious believers – for example, the Old Testament prophets, or Christian radical reformers such as Martin Luther King – are sometimes prepared to go against the norms and laws of society and even to reject it.

- Durkheim's thesis was modelled on primitive aboriginal societies and is therefore not a true reflection of modern religious belief and practice, which is more sophisticated and varied.

- Whilst society constantly changes, beliefs about the nature of God are timeless and unchanging. In many cases, religion resists the changing nature of society's beliefs.

However, some of Durkheim's observations are clearly relevant and appropriate. In many religious communities, most notably the conservative, evangelical and fundamentalist communities, commitment to the community is of primary importance and failure to live up to the moral and spiritual expectations of the group can lead only to exclusion. A recent example of this is the case of Ted Haggard, the senior pastor of the New Life Church in Colorado, and president of the National Association of Evangelicals. A high profile pastor, in November 2006 he was removed from

Taking it further...

Durkheim argued that religious phenomena emerge in any society when a separation is made between the sphere of the **profane** – the realm of everyday utilitarian activities – and the sphere of the **sacred** – those things which pertain to the numinous, the transcendental, the extraordinary. An object is intrinsically neither sacred nor profane. It becomes one or the other depending on how humans choose to consider it – as having utilitarian value alone or as having certain intrinsic attributes that have nothing to do with its instrumental value.

Ted Haggard, the man at the centre of the Colorado church scandal

his positions after revelations that he had employed the services of a gay prostitute from whom he had procured drugs. Three months later, in February 2007, after receiving prayer and counselling, Haggard issued a statement that he was 'completely heterosexual'. The claim was received with some concern by gay and lesbian movements in the US, suggesting as it did that homosexuality was a condition from which an individual could be 'cured'. This debate aside, Haggard had no choice but to attend counselling as part of the settlement he reached with the New Life Church, which also demanded that he should not speak publicly about the scandal, should reveal the amount of the financial settlement made, and should move from Colorado Springs. Such was the power of the church community to which he belonged and which he himself had founded, that even as (or perhaps because he was) a nationally-famous evangelical leader, he was forced to accept its sanctions and control.

Karl Marx

Marx argued that God was an invention of the human mind in order to satisfy emotional needs, declaring that 'the first requisite for the happiness of the people is the abolition of religion'. He believed that the ruling classes used religion to dominate and oppress their subjects by offering them an illusion of escape – 'It eased pain even as it created fantasies'. He was convinced that 'religion is so fully determined by economics that it is pointless to consider any of its doctrines or beliefs on their own merits'. He observed that man created God, not vice versa, and that religion was an alienating force, prescribing to God powers that man in fact possessed. Man had therefore lost control of his destiny through his belief in God.

Marx maintained that when a revolution overthrew the ruling class, and religion was abolished, the oppressed masses could be liberated. Only by loving one another rather than loving God could man reclaim his humanity. Ironically, religion had originated in revolutionary movements but, once detached from its roots, it had been used by the ruling classes to dominate and oppress. Inequality was legitimised in the name of religion, discouraging the subject classes from recognising their real situation and seeking to rise above it. Although religion offered a release from distress, it was a false release and thus, claimed Marx, was 'the opiate of the people'. Whilst giving nothing of true value, it promised salvation from bondage and misery in the after-life, where people would be rewarded for their virtue. Meanwhile, only supernatural intervention would solve problems on earth, with religion serving to justify the social order and a person's place within it, diverting attention away from the real source of social oppression and keeping the ruling classes in power.

In envisaging a non-religious community which would follow from revolution, Marx conceived of primitive communist societies in which the members of the community owned all resources jointly. People would have duties and roles, but their work would be an extension of their personality and would be inherently fulfilling to them, while at the same time contributing to the good of the entire community. In such a system, goods would be shared throughout the group, so that each person had what they needed to live (food, clothing, shelter) and to be productive (raw materials), but no more. In such a society religion would no longer be needed to fulfill the function that a capitalist society forced upon it.

Taking it further...

In the 19th century, Sunday schools attracted many children. Their aim was to produce citizens who were controlled and disciplined and accepted their social place. The children sang hymns which reinforced their place in society, including the famous *All Things Bright and Beautiful*.

This verse is no long found in regular hymn books:
The rich man in his castle,
The poor man at his gate,
God made them high and lowly
And ordered their estate.

Workers in the gold mines in Russia are shot dead by troops for striking, in 1912

Criticisms of Marx's view

- In most societies, the separation between church and state is far greater than Marx assumed.

- **Liberation theology**, in areas where there is considerable poverty, such as South America, has blended Marxism and Christianity in an attempt to change the nature of society for the oppressed without rejecting belief in God. The origins of the movement came from the experience of extreme poverty found in Latin America – an area that had been deeply Christian for centuries. The liberation theologians declared that such suffering was against the will of God and contrary to the teaching of Christ. Gustavo Gutierrez remarked: 'We are on the side of the poor, not because they are good, but because they are poor' (*A Theology of Liberation*, SCM, 2001), a view contrary to the traditional Marxist approach.

- Religion is a force that is open to interpretation, so it can be an influence for both change and stagnation. The internal philosophies of some religions may appear to discourage change, whilst other more radical branches encourage it. The biblical picture of God is of a deity who transforms situations and lifts up the oppressed.

- Weber suggested that religion promoted social change and that capitalism had developed in Europe due to the Protestant ethic of hard work and self-denial.

- Friedrich Engels, although himself a Marxist, did observe that the early Christian church offered a radical challenge to the governing Roman authorities, whilst Jesus himself is thought by some to have had Zealot (revolutionary) sympathies.

- Religion is no longer necessary in a capitalist society and yet it still exists. Whilst wealth is no longer held in the hands of a few ruling individuals but in corporations and conglomerates, religion may decline for other reasons (philosophical, rational) but not because the capitalist system preserves it.

Taking it further...

The papacy of John Paul II was suspicious of the liberation theology movement and its alleged Marxist connections. In the Puebla Conference of Bishops in 1979, the Pope declared that: '... those who sup with Marxism should use a long spoon'.

Taking it further...

Paul Tillich argued that religion encompasses that to which people are most devoted or that from which they expect to get the most fundamental satisfaction in life. It does not necessarily have to involve places of worship, doctrines or clergy. It can be anything to which people devote themselves that fills their lives with meaning.

Psychological critiques

Sigmund Freud

Freud argued that religion is a **projective system**, a 'universal neurosis' or illusion, which man should 'disregard in its relation to reality'. God, therefore, has no reality, but is a creation of the human mind. Like Durkheim, Freud saw the origins of religious belief as lying with primitive tribes. The tension between the dominant male and the subordinate males (sons) culminates in the overthrow of the father (a manifestation of the Oedipus complex), but the subsequent guilt of the sons leads them to elevate his memory and to worship him. The **super-ego** then takes the place of the father as a source of internalised authority, which is derived from the family, education and the church. It represses anti-social impulses such as killing and, by inducing fear and guilt, it is crucial for civilisation. It is this we call the conscience, and God is not only a father substitute, but also a projection of the super-ego. Freud maintained that man was dependent upon religion to 'make his helplessness tolerable', and that whilst he maintained this unhealthy dependency he would never be truly happy.

Sigmund Freud

Freud repeatedly observed that guilt plays a fundamental role in the psyche, and that it mainly operates unconsciously. Guilt, in Freud's thinking, must have had an original reason: at one point there must have been a violation of a law, which created the sense of guilt. In his reasoning, Freud takes recourse in an anthropological theory of his time, which claims that at the origin there was a murder of the primal father. This murder is the motivation for the development of law and therefore functions as the origin of all father-religions, primarily the monotheistic religions, which are essentially law based.

A number of different psychological motives underlying religious impulses are discussed throughout Freud's works. A principal element for Freud was the feeling of helplessness in the face of external dangers, inner impulses, death and society. Freud made much of the similarities between religious rituals and obsessional rituals (for example, the compulsive need to wash your hands in a specific way or on specific occasions). These function to protect the ego from fantasies, desires and especially sexual impulses which are normally repressed. Religious rituals, he believed, operate in the same way.

Criticisms of Freud's view

- Freud attributed all religious behaviour to the projection of psychosexual drives and claimed that the individual's relation to God depended on their relationship with their father. However, Nelson and Jones (1957) found that the concept of God correlated more highly with a person's relationship with their mother than with their father.

- Kate Lowenthal distinguished between **projective** religion, which is immature, and **intrinsic** religion, which is serious and reflective. Freud assumed that all aspects of belief in God were immature, and he neglected the diversity and development of religious beliefs.

- Arthur Guirdham argued that Freud overplayed the connection between belief in God and the psychopathological tendencies of much organised religion, and between the feeling of security in the womb (the **oceanic feeling**) and religious belief. He observed that Freud's anti-religious stance may be thought just as neurotic as the religious preoccupations of others.

- Freud strived to be objective, although by current standards the methods he used probably allowed his biases to influence his data. His influence in psychology has declined over the years, and his theories of the primal horde have been rejected as mere conjecture. Peter Moore observes: 'Most post-Freudians think his need to explain everything (art, religion, ethics, society) by sex tells us more about his obsessional neuroses than ours'.

Carl Jung

Jung was Freud's pupil, but left Freud's following when they disagreed over the relative importance of sexuality and spirituality to a person's psychological development: Freud emphasised sexuality over spirituality; Jung disagreed.

Jung was concerned with the interplay between conscious and unconscious forces. He proposed two kinds of unconscious: personal and collective. The **personal unconscious** (shadow) includes those things about ourselves that we would like to forget. The **collective unconscious** refers to events that we all share, by virtue of having a common heritage (humanity). For example, the image (archetype) of a mythic hero is something that is present in all cultures, and they are often viewed as gods.

Taking it further...

Despite the fact that Freud framed his ideas about religion in a general way, what he said can only really apply to traditional monotheistic religions such as Christianity, Judaism, and Islam. Polytheistic religions, pantheistic religions, and even religions which focus on a mother goddess are not susceptible to his criticisms.

Jung was fascinated with non-Western religious perspectives, and sought to find some common ground between East and West. In doing so, he had a very broad view of what it means to be empirical. Suppose, for example, that I hear a voice, which I think to be God's, but that you (sitting beside me) do not, it would be an empirical observation for Jung. For most contemporary scientists, however, it would not be considered an empirical observation and, because this is a decisive area of disagreement, far less research has been done on Jungian approaches to religion than on the Freudian perspective.

Most importantly, Jung maintained that religion is essential for a balanced psyche, arguing that it integrates the personality, quite the contrary to Freud's view that it leads to neurotic dysfunction.

Popularist critiques

A popularist critique of religion aims to identify the obvious negative and, in some cases, alarming features of religion past and present, and to persuade the layman as well as the scholar that religious belief is dangerous, outmoded and ridiculous. A leading figure in promoting this kind of critique is Richard Dawkins. Dawkins has become a popular media figure, regularly speaking out on religious issues, giving the uncompromising atheistic position whether the issue under debate is the Asian Tsunami of 2004 or another round in the ring over the creation versus evolution dispute. His Channel Four programme *The Root of all Evil?*, broadcast in January 2006, reinforced his position (with his supporters and his detractors) as the UK's leading atheist, and his campaign against religion came to a head with the publication of his book *The God Delusion* in October 2006. Interestingly, *The Root of all Evil?* quickly became virtually a cult documentary, earning its own extensive entry in Wikipedia.

Dawkins is a scientist by profession, and the holder of the Charles Simonyi Chair in the Public Understanding of Science at Oxford University. As an evolutionary biologist, his work first came to prominence with the publication in 1976 of *The Selfish Gene*. Since then, he has published eight further books, including *The Blind Watchmaker* (1986), *Climbing Mount Improbable* (1996) and *The Ancestor's Tale* (2004). However, it is indisputable that it is as a professional atheist (not unlike David Hume and Bertrand Russell) that Dawkins has gained celebrity, being loved or hated with the passion that he himself demonstrates over what he perceives to be the dangerous implications of religion and religious thinking.

Dawkins is perhaps more accurately described as an **antitheist**: he does not simply espouse atheism as a personal ideology, leaving religious believers to the comforts and insights of their faith. Rather, as he tells Mark Dowd in the Channel Four documentary, *Tsunami: Where was God?* (December 2005), 'I want people to stop believing'. However, despite his public acclaim, is Richard Dawkins' fervent desire to prevent the spread of the 'virus of religion' as he calls it, reasonable?

Dawkins' objections to religious belief

Dawkins' objections to religious belief fall broadly under four headings:

1 Religious belief is not necessary
Firstly, he argues (and he is by no means alone in this) that a Darwinian world view makes belief in God unnecessary. He dismisses the belief that there is

Richard Dawkins

any ultimate, mystical significance in the world or human beings, arguing instead that the fact that humans exist at all is a remarkable enough coincidence of biology without looking for any greater significance. Dawkins' position as a biologist is not surprising – biology universally accepts evolution as the explanation for all living things, and evidence against evolution is extremely thin – but beyond this he uses it to further his atheist agenda.

2 Faith claims

Beliefs about the divine creation of the world are essentially faith claims, and Dawkins argues that the faith claims of religion are a retreat from an evidence-based quest for the truth. 'Faith is the great cop out, the great excuse to evade the need to think and evaluate the evidence,' he observes in *The Nullifidian*, Vol. 1, No. 8, 1994. He furthers this by arguing that religion offers an **impoverished world view**: 'The universe presented by organised religion is a poky little mediaeval universe' (*The Third Culture,* ed. John Brockman, Touchstone, 1996). In other words, Dawkins claims, supernatural explanations of the world prevent us from investigating further. If we are satisfied to explain the world in terms of God, there is no need to ask any further questions and to discover more about the universe.

3 The issue of purpose

The question of purpose and significance should be an ongoing question, the answer to which, Dawkins suggests, lies in humanity itself. Humans are purpose-driven beings, who assume purpose in the universe because we are driven to invest purpose in everything we do. However, to assume that the purpose and meaning of the world are to be found outside the world and humanity is, he claims, an unwarranted assumption which closes the door on further investigation. 'Growing up in the universe ... also means growing out of parochial and supernatural views of the universe ... not copping out with superstitious ideas' (Royal Institution Christmas Lectures, 1991).

4 The virus of religion

Fourthly – and it is this view which has gained Dawkins much recent media attention – he argues that religion leads to evil, likening it to a malignant virus which infects human minds. He dismisses religious faith as: 'An indulgence of irrationality that is nourishing extremism, division and terror' (*The Root of all Evil?*, January 2006). Dawkins draws on a range of evidence, but he is particularly concerned with the beliefs and practices of fundamentalist Islam and evangelical Christianity, which he associates (not always unreasonably) with misleading education (teaching creationism on an equal scientific footing with evolution in faith schools), prejudice and ignorance, inciting fear, and 'child abuse'. Dawkins proposes a classic critique of the relationship between religion and morality which is not exclusive to him, but he furthers this by asserting that it is a form of child abuse to refer to the children of Christian or Muslim parents as a 'Christian child' or a 'Muslim child'. Perhaps more importantly, however, he links the events of 9/11 and 7/7 with religiously-motivated terrorism, a powerful and emotive basis on which to launch a strong attack on the influence of religion in the modern world.

What does the 9/11 disaster tell us about God and moral evil?

Extremism

So how convincing are Dawkins' arguments? Firstly, it is fair to say that he correctly identifies some of the more alarming examples of religious extremism. In *The Root of all Evil?* Dawkins visits a Hell House Outreach presentation in Colorado, a graphic series of crudely acted scenes in which homosexuals, women who have had an abortion, and a drunken teenager who was responsible for the death of his girlfriend in a car crash, are all shown as heading straight for Hell. He talks to a friend of Paul Hill, the American pastor idolised by the Army of God for his murder of an abortionist, who calmly suggests that it would not be against biblical principles were the state to execute adulterers. Interestingly, he visits the New Life Church in Colorado, where the recently disgraced Ted Haggard (see page 31) was at the time Senior Pastor. Despite Haggard's powerful position (Dawkins says that he held regular conference calls with George W. Bush), in November 2006 Haggard admitted to his involvement in homosexual sex, and was dismissed from his post at the New Life Church and from his leadership of the National Association of Evangelicals. Revelations of this kind are only grist to Dawkins' mill. However, as A. N. Wilson observes, Dawkins goes in search of 'the grotesques in the Middle East and the Bible belt of America, and has no difficulty in making them seem absurd' (*Daily Mail*, 9th March 2007).

Dawkins the fundamentalist

In response to Dawkins' arguments, Melvin Tinker observes that 'Dawkins exhibits all the hallmarks of those forms of religion he so despises: vehemence, narrow-mindedness and intolerance. He is a 'fundamentalist of the scientific kind' *(Dawkins' Dilemmas* in *The Briefing*, Issue 337, October 2006).

Tinker suggests that Dawkins' claim that religion is a mental virus does not bear close scrutiny. Dawkins explains his belief by reference to **memes** (Dawkins' own term) – ideas or beliefs which are analogous to genes (the hereditary material which determines our physical characteristics). Memes spread rapidly from one person to another, infecting people's minds, Dawkins claims, especially in families. Tinker suggests that the analogy is false, observing that genes which are biologically transmitted cannot be changed once the process of reproduction is underway. Ideas, however, can be changed – we can reassess them at any stage in our life.

Furthermore, Tinker argues, Dawkins' notion of memes is self-defeating. If religious belief is a meme, passed through infection from one to another, so too is Dawkins' atheism. Even the idea of a meme is a meme! In this way, Tinker is implying that Dawkins' memes are **bliks** (R. M. Hare's famous term) – ways of looking at the world which cannot be falsified whatever evidence is presented to the contrary. It seems unlikely that Dawkins' atheistic meme is any more likely to be falsified in his mind than the beliefs of the religious fundamentalist he attacks.

Ontological reductionism

Tinker also criticises Dawkins for reducing everything to scientific terms, a process called **ontological reductionism.** Dawkins argues that the sole reason for living is to pass on DNA; Tinker observes that, although it is undeniable that biological organisms do pass on their DNA to their offspring, it is by no means their sole purpose. In Dawkins' defence, he does address this issue in the documentary *The Big Question* (2004), in which he states the case that humans are breaking Darwin's rules. We pursue hobbies, explore the world, have sex for non-reproductive purposes, and develop machines which have nothing to do with survival.

Taking it further...

History shows that many intellectuals can undergo dramatic changes in perspective. For example, in 2004, the renowned atheist Antony Flew began to express deist opinions and, although he has not been specific about what he now believes, he received considerable criticism for his change in position.

Nevertheless, Dawkins is on shaky ground when he claims that the universe we see is one which has 'no purpose, no evil and no other good, nothing but blind, pitiless indifference… DNA neither knows nor cares. And we dance to its music' (*River Out of Eden: A Darwinian View of Life*, Basic Books, 1995). If this is the case, Tinker argues, 'the logical upshot of this is that the Yorkshire Ripper danced to the music of his DNA' (*The Briefing*) – in other words, he was not accountable for his actions because it was in his DNA, something over which we have little or no control.

Tinker suggests that the greatest irony is that Dawkins' writings have something of a religious feel to them, as he employs mythological language to convey his ideas. For example, he describes genes as 'Chicago gangsters' the predominant quality of which is 'ruthless selfishness' as they 'leap from body to body down the generations… The genes are immortals… By dictating the way survival machines and their nervous systems are built, genes exert ultimate power over behaviour' (*The Selfish Gene,* Oxford University Press, 1989). Tinker observes that selfishness is, of course, normally understood as a moral quality and therefore seems quite inappropriate as a term to describe particles of DNA.

Tinker addresses Dawkins' accusation that religion is harmful: 'He makes a value judgement that extremism and terror are 'bad' things, but bad for whom?' Tinker asks. 'Not for the terrorists who get their way and pass on their genes' (*The Briefing*). Finally, Tinker demands that Dawkins be more precise when he talks about religion. Dawkins' sweeping statements suggest that everything he says about religion applies equally to them all, as 'intellectually irresponsible as lumping all animals together and saying that what goes for elephants must go for ants' (*The Briefing*). Rather, it is easy to see that each religion must be judged on its own terms and, within each religion, each denomination, faction or splinter group.

A. N. Wilson, although himself capable of the most acerbic attacks on religious belief, asks 'Why in God's name, do we take this silly, shallow scientist seriously?' (*Daily Mail*, 9th March). He describes Dawkins as 'an arch simplifier, a hurler of unnecessary insults' and notes that Dawkins assumes that God *should* be provable by evidence, but misses the point that, along with many everyday experiences, God is not someone for whom a scientist *needs* to provide evidence. Belief in God is not stupid, but thinking we could prove God by scientific experiment would be: 'By saying that he won't believe anything that can't be provided in a science lesson, Richard Dawkins lines himself up with the more nerdish sort of first year Philosophy students and leaflet distributors at Hyde Park Corner.'

Dawkins' ideas are certainly interesting, and he raises many important points about religion, not only in the present day, but over human history. It is undeniably the case that religion has caused pain and misery, but so too have many other institutions which have fallen into human hands. Dawkins' approach is intended to shock, as the claims of religion have doubtless shocked and dismayed many atheists and agnostics – but also sincere believers who have seen beliefs and practices emerge in the name of God, which are, at the least, counter-intuitive. Dawkins argues charismatically, if not always soundly, and it is clear that his influence on British intellectual culture will continue for some time to come.

Taking it further...

Mary Midgeley points out that to speak of genes as being selfish is as nonsensical as speaking of atoms being jealous! (*Genes and Juggling*, in *Philosophy* 54, 1979). Ironically, Dawkins' quasi-religious language harks back to the pagan language which spoke of Mars as the god of war.

Taking it further...

A. N. Wilson claims: 'No one of any imagination can fail to doubt the conventional ideas about God from time to time. The Bible is full of anguished questioning of God. The history of the human relationship with God is by no means all one of comfort.'

Other arguments for the non-existence of God

- The problem of evil could be seen to be the strongest atheistic argument. For a full discussion of this topic, see pages 41–55 in the AS textbook in this series. If you choose to take this approach in your A2 exam, you must make sure that you examine it from the perspective of the problem rather than the solutions. Extensive discussion of the classical theodicies will not highlight how this evidential critique offers a serious challenge to belief in God.

- Science and rationalism have made a significant contribution to atheistic belief since the Enlightenment. It is possible to explain the world both religiously and non-religiously and therefore the existence of God cannot be decisively proved by referring to the evidence provided by the natural world.

- A strong moral case against the existence of God can also be offered. For a full discussion of this, see pages 73–83 in the Ethics section.

- Modernism rejects the literal use and understanding of many religious terms, such as 'heaven', 'hell' or 'demons', claiming that they are merely representations of out-dated mythological concepts.

- Advances in biblical criticism and analysis, which have discouraged a literal interpretation of the text and revealed the writers' use of sources and the way in which they had been influenced by their cultural environment, could give grounds to argue that the Bible cannot therefore contribute in any way to proving the existence of God.

Can God be disproved?

If it is not possible to prove decisively the existence of God, it must also be impossible to disprove it. It is questionable whether the atheist really is on any stronger ground than the theist, bearing in mind that the same rules of proof and probability must apply to an atheistic argument as to a theistic one. The biblical writers did not countenance the possibility of atheism or suggest that it may have any intellectual or philosophical credibility: it is 'the fool' who has 'said in his heart there is no God' (Psalm 10:4; 53:1). However, theists may argue that even within theistic belief there remains an element of agnosticism, since the transcendent God is ultimately unknowable and cannot be presumed to be known fully.

Is theism stronger than atheism?

The principle of Ockham's Razor

Ockham's Razor, associated with William of Ockham (1285–1349), is the principle that, in trying to understand something, getting unnecessary information out of the way is the fastest way to the truth or the best explanation: 'What can be done with fewer assumptions is done in vain with more' or 'Entities should not be multiplied unnecessarily'. Ockham was well known for his insistence on the careful use of language as a tool for thinking and for using observation as a tool for testing reality. The principle is considered to have laid the groundwork for modern scientific enquiry.

Taking it further...

The resulting **law of parsimony** or **simplicity** goes back to Aristotle, who claimed that nature operates in the shortest possible way. In other words, nature operates efficiently, using as few steps as necessary to fulfil its purpose.

Taking it further...

Stephen Hawking takes the principle of Ockham's Razor a stage further:

'We could still imagine a set of laws that determines events completely for some supernatural being, who could observe the present state of the universe without disturbing it. However, such models of the universe are not of much interest to us mortals. It seems better to employ the principle known as Ockham's Razor and cut out all the features of the theory which cannot be observed' (Stephen Hawking, *A Brief History of Time*).

Ockham used the principle to argue against attempts to justify the existence of God by reason alone, declaring that the matter of God's existence could only ever be known by faith, not proof.

The need for explanation

Theism is a system of belief which attempts to provide an explanation for certain phenomena in the world: the existence of something rather than nothing; the nature of the world, its character and possible purpose; the place and significance of human beings. Belief in God is not *just* that, but it is a significant part of it.

• Why look for an explanation?
The universe is religiously ambiguous – the existence of God is not overwhelmingly obvious (the **epistemic distance**) and the universe itself is not self-explanatory. We are therefore aware that people *do* hold different explanations for the universe and the place of humanity, even though those explanations may be contradictory.

• Are explanations important?
The human quest for explanation inevitably and rightly seeks for the ultimate explanation of everything observable – that object or objects on which everything else depends for its existence and properties... A may be explained by B, and B by C, but in the end there will be some one object on whom all other objects depend. We will have to acknowledge **something** *as ultimate – the great metaphysical issue is* **what** *that is.* (Richard Swinburne, *Is There a God?*, Oxford University Press, 1996)

• Is it reasonable to expect to find an explanation?
In the 1948 radio debate between Bertrand Russell and F. C. Copleston, they raised the question of how far it is necessary to trace an explanation back for it to be a complete explanation:

Russell: But when is an explanation adequate? Suppose I am about to make a flame with a match. You may say that the adequate explanation of that is that I rub it on the box.
Copleston: Well, for practical purposes – but theoretically, that is only a partial explanation. An adequate explanation must ultimately be a total explanation, to which nothing further can be added
Russell: Then I can only say you're looking for something which can't be got, and which one ought not expect to get.

Copleston, a supporter of the cosmological argument, maintained that a complete explanation of the universe may not always be practically necessary, but is theoretically possible and interesting. For Copleston, it is therefore reasonable to seek God as a necessary explanation for things.

• The psychological dimension
Man's need to find an explanation for things which puzzle him suggests that we are not satisfied with saying that things 'just are'. Keith Ward observes that, if the scientist were asked 'Why does water boil when it is heated?', no one would be satisfied with the answer 'There is no reason, it just does'. There are problems about the world that both believers and non-believers feel a need to explain, most especially the **problem of evil** and **questions of existence and nature**, and to say that there is no explanation is neither intellectually nor psychologically satisfactory.

Does theism multiply entities without necessity?

A theistic explanation of the universe makes two basic assumptions:

- that supernatural forces exist which are powerful enough to influence the lives of individuals and the destiny of the whole universe

- that human beings can communicate with these beings and enter into a relationship with them.

An atheistic explanation will seek to explain the same features of the world but without supernatural inference, and can argue that the theistic explanation is unnecessarily complicated. A theistic view of the universe *does* necessitate belief in more than one supernatural, omnipotent being and can lead to **saving theism by adding hypotheses** such as:

- life after death, angels and demons

- theodicy and the danger of qualification: 'A fine brash hypothesis may thus be killed by inches, the death by a thousand qualifications' (Anthony Flew)

- miracles, religious experience and the mysterious nature of God.

Further problems

1 The complexity of theistic systems may be increased by looking at the functions which they themselves may serve and their consequences:

- to control society and ensure the submission of certain social groups

- to justify war, terror and oppression

- to justify morality, law and punishment.

2 The range of reasons given by people for *why* they believe in God is vast. James Sire (*Why Should Anyone Believe Anything at All?*) conducted a survey amongst US university students, which revealed reasons such as: parents, friends, society, culture, the search for identity, comfort, the 'feel good factor', direct and personal experience of God and Jesus, the Bible, miracles, 'because it's true', 'it's logical'. Of them all, he identified 'because it gives the best explanation for the tough issues of life' as the most compelling reason offered – as long as it meets the highest standards of self-consistency and we have made a genuine attempt to find the truth.

3 In defence of theism as the best explanation:

- Nobody is a non-believer: 'The scientist has faith in nature and himself' (John Blanchard, *Does God Believe in Atheists?* Evangelical Press, 2000).

- Why should theism be less intellectually acceptable than atheism? 'All questions about existence will reveal the need for God' (John Blanchard, ibid.).

- Is atheism itself scientifically proven?

- Can science explain everything?

4 What about Ockham's Razor?
Thomas Aquinas anticipated the challenge of Ockham's Razor as offered by the atheist in the preface to the **Five Ways**: 'It is superfluous to suppose that

Taking it further...

'So there is our universe. It is characterised by vast, all-persuasive temporal order, the conformity of nature to formula, recorded in the scientific laws formulated by humans… These phenomena are clearly things too big for science to explain… Note that I am not postulating a 'God of the gaps', a God merely to explain the things which science has not yet explained. I am postulating a God to explain what science explains; I do not deny that science explains, but I postulate God to explain why science explains.' (Richard Swinburne, *Is There a God?*)

what can be accounted for by a few principles has been produced by many. But it seems that everything we see in the world can be accounted for by other principles, supposing God did not exist. For all natural things can be reduced to one principle, which is nature, and all voluntary things can be reduced to one principle which is human reason or will...' However, he solved this dilemma by his observation that neither nature nor human will could act without the agency of a 'higher agent'.

Philip Gibbs observes: 'Simplicity is subjective and the universe does not always have the same ideas about simplicity as we do. Successful theorists often speak of symmetry and beauty as well as simplicity... The law of parsimony is no substitute for insight... it should never be relied upon to make or defend a conclusion' (cited in Blanchard, ibid.).

CHAPTER 2
Selected problems in the philosophy of religion

2.1 Life after death

Key Ideas

- The nature of death and post-mortem existence

- The relationship between the body and the mind/soul

- Near-death experiences and parapsychology

- Reincarnation and rebirth

- Resurrection and the immortality of the soul

The nature of death and post-mortem existence

'The undiscover'd country from whose bourn no traveller returns' (*Hamlet*, William Shakespeare)

Our earthly life will end one day because, by their very nature, physical things perish. The question is whether or not there is life after death (post-mortem existence) and if so, what is it like? For human beings generally, the prospect of life after death is a desirable one for a number of reasons:

- We are scared of death. It can make us sad, angry and frightened and the prospect of an after life makes it easier to bear.

- It is hard to accept that this short life is all that there is. We feel that there has to be something beyond this life, which gives meaning to our limited earthly existence.

- The moral law is only fulfilled when the good are rewarded and the evil punished. Since this doesn't always happen in our earthly life, an after life, overseen by a moral commander, must be necessary. 'Multitudes who sleep in the dust of the earth will awake: some to everlasting life, others to shame and everlasting contempt' (Daniel 12:2).

- The after life would be the place where human potential could ultimately be realised.

- Religious believers often claim that life is a holy and precious gift from God (the sanctity of life). It is difficult to think of something of such high value ending so quickly. There must be more than one brief lifetime in which to fulfil our relationship with God.

Taking it further...

The Bible talks of an after life as a gift from God, shown in the resurrection of Jesus: '... that which has been begun by God during man's life on earth ... will be continued and completed by God, in his own time and in his own ways, beyond the confines of earthly life (Robert McAfee Brown, *A Handbook of Christian Theology*, Fontana, 1960).

- Eastern religions speak of reincarnation – the belief that the soul moves after death to another body, until it is finally released into a higher form. The **Dhammapada** states: 'Like a fish which is thrown on dry land, taken from his home in the waters, the mind strives and struggles to get free from the power of Death'.

- 'If the human potential is to be fulfilled in the lives of individuals, these lives must be prolonged far beyond the limits of our present bodily existence' (*Christianity at the Centre*, John Hick, Macmillan, 1968).

Arguments against the concept of an after life

Yet for other people, there is no post-mortem existence. Death is a biological function and a necessary part of the natural process. Human beings, like all animals, will one day die – and when the body dies, the consciousness and personality dies with it. In *What I Believe* (Routledge 1989), Bertrand Russell wrote: 'I believe that when I die I shall rot, and nothing of my ego will survive.'

So, for some people, the notion of life after death is meaningless and unnecessary. The clear physical evidence of the destruction of the body at death makes it logically impossible to speak of an after life, since it would involve a contradiction of everything that empirical evidence appears to support. To sustain this view, it is necessary to find no overwhelming reason to claim that the prospect of an after life makes the contingency of this life bearable. To reject belief in an after life is to accept that there is no more meaning to human existence outside the physical boundaries of earthly existence, or at least that the notion of post-mortem existence can be limited to the notion of living on in the memories of loved ones, or in our achievements while on earth. In *The Root of all Evil?* (Channel Four, 2006), Richard Dawkins poses the question of why it is necessary to have religious faith in order to find something important and significant in life. 'We are so grotesquely lucky to be here,' he claims. The exact combination of factors – biological, geographical, ancestral and social – which result, in Dawkins' words, 'in a me or you', is highly improbable. We may as easily – more easily, in fact – have not existed than existed. This is enough, he claims, for us to value life as intrinsically special; there is no need to ask for more beyond this life.

Even the language of the after life poses problems for some scholars. For the empiricist, to speak at all of a soul is a meaningless exercise, since there are no observations that can be made which make it possible to verify its existence. A. J. Ayer claimed 'that (to say) there is something imperceptible inside a man, which is his soul or his real self, and that it goes on living after he is dead' (*Language, Truth and Logic*, 1936) is, therefore, a meaningless claim. Other scholars have highlighted the incomprehensibility of such talk, arguing that the very phrase 'life after death' entails an impossible contradiction since life and death are two mutually exclusive states. As in a plane crash, there are those who die and those who survive, there are no 'dead survivors', a logical impossibility which is tantamount to what life after death involves.

For other thinkers, however, the notion of an after life is meaningful and conceivable, but need not be contingent upon the action of a loving and omnipotent God who, in some way, recreates personal identity beyond the

Taking it further...

John Hick observes: 'In each present moment God, unseen, is seeking our response. The call to respond to God is immediate and urgent—not because the doors of salvation are going to be shut at the moment of death but because the discovery of God means also our own fulfilment and joy.' (*Death and Eternal Life*, Westminster, 1994).

death process. Rather, the nature of human beings is that their energy continues beyond the death of the physical body, and they can continue to be experienced in a real way by those who have the power to communicate with them. The modern interest in non-theistic spirituality embraces this idea, although for theistic believers it is a dangerous way to think of the after life, as something separate from the love and power of God who calls all people to be accountable to him in this life in order to determine how they will spend eternity.

The relationship between the body and the mind/soul

For those who believe in a post-mortem existence, the most important issue is *what* exactly survives death and lives on. This depends on what is meant by a 'person' and the key to this is to understand the relationship between the mind and the body:

- The **monistic** view is that the body and mind are linked together to form one entity.

- The **dualistic** view is that the body and mind are distinct and separate entities, though each can influence the other.

- Within this, there are different dualistic views. The first is that the mind depends totally on the body in order to function.

- The second is that the mind and bodily influence each other equally, but that the two need each other in order to be conscious and aware of the world.

- The third view is that body and mind are distinct entities that are mysteriously locked together in this world, but that the soul will escape and live on after the death of the body.

The mind and the soul may be the same thing. The terms refer to the thinking, feeling, willing and thoughtful consciousness and self-awareness of a person. It is more than just the inner workings of the brain; it is also the source of creativity, ideas and imagination. Moreover, the soul has, in religious terms, a unique value – each person has an individual soul, possibly created by God, which is their real self and makes them a truly unique individual.

So, if there is a post-mortem existence, does this suggest the survival of the physical body or the survival just of the soul or, indeed, the survival of both body and soul? When we think, for example, of great writers or scientists such as Shakespeare or Einstein, it is not their bodies that we think of, but their minds. However, without their body, could we speak of them actually existing?

The monistic view

In the monistic view, human beings are psycho-physical unities. A person is made up of the physical body – which walks, talks, sleeps and so on – and the mind, which determines mental behaviour and characteristics and displays such qualities as intelligence and humour. There is no soul/ mind that is distinct from the body and which survives death. 'Man does not have a

Are ideas of Hell purely mythological?

Taking it further...

In *Death and Eternal Life* (Westminster, 1994), John Hick suggests that the mind and brain are separate entities which may act upon each other, but act in a different way: '… mind is a reality of a different kind from matter … mind and brain are independent but interacting realities'.

body, he is a body … he is flesh-animated-by-soul, the whole conceived as a psycho-physical unity' (J. A. T. Robinson, *A Handbook of Christian Theology*, Fontana, 1960).

The dualistic view

In the dualistic view, however, the physical body and the spiritual soul are regarded as distinct entities. Human beings have composite natures – partly material (physical body) and partly non-material (mind/soul). Gilbert Ryle, in *The Concept of the Mind* (Penguin, 1949), spoke of the 'ghost in a machine', that is, the 'ghost' of the mind in the 'machine' of the body. For Ryle, body and soul/ mind are one and the same and he advocates **philosophical behaviourism** – the notion that all mental events are really physical events interpreted in a mental way. To speak of body and soul is, therefore, a category error, akin to separating the university from its buildings, or the relatives from the family.

René Descartes said that the body is spatial but not conscious, whilst the mind is non-spatial and conscious, with feelings and thoughts. He argued that the body and mind are separate but interact with each other through the workings of the brain. When the physical body dies, the soul lives on. In *Discourse on the Method* (edit. Penguin, 1970), he wrote: 'Our soul is of a nature entirely independent of the body, and consequently … it is not bound to die with it. And since we cannot see any other causes that destroy the soul, we are naturally led to conclude that it is immortal'.

Both the monistic and dualistic views present difficulties, most notably about whether or not the physical body is, in some way, linked to the soul. If it is, then if only the soul survives death, a very important aspect of the human character is lost. If both body and soul are needed for eternal life, then how can the empirical evidence of physical death be explained? After much consideration, Bertrand Russell suggested that probably nothing survived: '… our mental life is bound up with brain structure and organised bodily energy. Therefore it is rational to suppose that mental life ceases when bodily life ceases' (*Russell on Religion*, Routledge, 1999).

Others disagree, however, saying that life after death is not only a possibility, but also a desirable prospect, which will require our personal identities either:

- to survive the death process

or:

- to be given a new mode of being with which to continue our existence.

Philosophers through the ages have suggested several avenues in which to seek for the answers to the question of whether or not there is life after death. The most significant are:

- Near-death experiences – do they provide any evidence of an after life?
- Parapsychology – can it offer any reliable insights into the possibility of post-mortem survival?

Four ways of understanding how personal identity can survive the death process may be broadly categorised into those characteristic of Eastern

Gilbert Ryle

Taking it further...

In *God and the Mind Machine*, John Puddeford (SPCK, 1996) suggests that the characteristics of the mind/soul include **qualia** (sensory experiences such as taste) and **intentionality** or **aboutness**, i.e. I don't just *think*, I think *about something*.

Taking it further...

Some scholars have attempted to address the dilemma of post-mortem existence by turning to **materialism** or **behaviourism**. This is the view that mental activity is, in fact, a physical thing – for instance, the feeling of emotion is just the interacting of chemicals in the physical body. In *Confessions of a Philosopher* (Phoenix, 1997), Bryan Magee commented: 'The human body is a single entity, one subject of behaviour and experience with a single history. We are not two entities mysteriously laced together. We have made what Ryle calls a category mistake'.

religions – reincarnation and rebirth – and those more commonly associated with monotheistic religious traditions – the immortality of the soul and the resurrection of the body.

Near-death experiences

A near-death experience is said to occur when someone dies for a short while, perhaps on the operating table, during a heart attack or in an accident, and is resuscitated before the state becomes irreversible. Many who have experienced this claim to have floated out of their bodies, travelled down a tunnel and arrived in a place of light where they encountered either a dead relative, or a religious figure from their own tradition. Hugh Montefiore defined them as 'something very specific which can occur when people are near to death, or think themselves to be. It is not uncommon for people to have … out of the ordinary experiences when they are … in situations close to death' (*The Paranormal – A Bishop Investigates*, 2002).

Raymond Moody famously made a study of these experiences in his work *The Light Beyond* (Bantam, 1998). He discovered many similarities in the testimonies of those who claim to have had such experiences and he was able to highlight a number of problems. For instance, experients could be dreaming, or remembering some lost subconscious memory (cryptomnesia), or they may be having a hallucination caused by a lack of oxygen to the brain.

Near-death experiences are individually unique, but appear to have a common pattern of 'core experiences'. K. Ring (*Life at Death*, 1982) identified these as an out-of-body experience, a feeling of peace, entering darkness and seeing light.

Peter Fenwick (*The Truth in the Light*, 1995) went on to identify several features which represent the 'full syndrome' of near-death experiences, including entering a tunnel, experiencing a barrier that marks the point of no return, visiting another country, meeting relatives, a life review, the decision to return, a rapid return to the physical body, and the subsequent removal of the fear of death.

• Feelings of peace

These may be due to drugs such as morphine, since such feelings can be induced without a near-death experience. Or it may be the release of endorphins to help the individual cope with the fear of death, or the hormone ACTH which helps cope with stress. Or maybe it is a foretaste of heaven? Since this cannot be tested, it is not a satisfactory explanation for those who are looking for a physical explanation.

• Out-of-body experiences

If the mind can exist without the brain, then such experiences are possible. However, they can be induced by psychedelic drugs or be psychologically induced. People often relate things seen and heard which would be inexplicable from the perspective of lying in a hospital bed. For example, a woman in hospital in Seattle reported seeing a tennis shoe lying on a window ledge on the third floor of the hospital, which was subsequently found to be the case (Montefiore, 2002). Are memories therefore processed from a bird's eye view? If so, why?

Taking it further...

A 1982 Gallup Poll found that 15% of respondents claimed to have had a near-death experience, and a study of cardiac patients at Southampton General Hospital found that 11% reported a near-death experience. Although some people may be more susceptible than others to the experience, no study has revealed any significant reason why any group should be more likely to experience one than another. Whilst such experiences seem to be part of ancient cultures – Plato refers to the soldier Er, who was killed in battle, but returned to describe his experience – scientific study of them has only recently become possible.

Can a near-death experience prove that there is an after life?

• The tunnel and the light

Does this mark the transition to another realm? Light is a frequently used metaphor for divine realities and holiness. Does it represent the birth process? If so, why? Is it the result of 'disinhibition and excitation of brain cells, especially in the visual cortex'? (Montefiore, 2002). This may lead to random firing of the cells in the visual cortex, giving the illusion of a rapid journey down a tunnel towards a brilliant light. However, the journey is not described by experients as random, but orderly.

• The being of light

This experience is most easily interpreted religiously – it is usually talked of as a positive, loving experience, beyond description. The figure is usually described as having great authority and who encourages and welcomes the experient. It is often, but not always, related to the individual's own religious culture – Fenwick describes a Roman Catholic who had a vision of three young Indian men.

• The barrier

This is the point beyond which visitors may not pass – variously described as 'a green trellis fence', 'a black, shiny, leather bench' or 'a door which began to open'. 'Perhaps, (for those who do believe that NDE is a spiritual journey), the barrier is an indication that our life is regulated by providence, and providence has decreed that it is not yet our time to die' (Montefiore, 2002).

• Another country

This is often described as an idyllic pastoral scene, filled with light, fragrance and colour – or a country beyond the barrier. Is it a symbolic representation of refreshment, peace and contentment linked with the image of heaven or paradise? Or is the experient consoling themselves with a well-loved place in their memory?

• Relatives and friends

Fenwick (1995) describes one such experience: 'Then I saw a group of people between me and the light. I knew them: my brother, who had died a few years before, was gesticulating delightedly as I approached'. Could this be a retreat from the fear of death to the comfort of known and loved ones? Montefiore suggests that 'it would be difficult to produce a physiological explanation of the experience'.

• Life review

This common component sometimes takes place in front of the being of light. Some feel they have been weighed up, others have a life preview and are told there are tasks awaiting them, which is why they need to return to the physical body. They also take place in other circumstances – e.g. air pilots approaching the speed of sound – and could, again, be explained as the result of anoxia – when the temporal lobe, through lack of oxygen, undergoes random firing and excitation. However, if this is so, why are the memories so orderly and clear? Religious interpretations are inclined to see this as a foretaste of the life review after death.

• The decision to return

Usually people want to stay in the experience but this is impossible and, once the decision to return is made, it is put immediately into effect. The anoxia explanation here would claim that it is due to the sudden re-supply of oxygen to the brain, whilst those who favour a religious interpretation suggest that divine providence has decreed that the spiritual journey must come to an end.

● **The return**

This is usually rapid and is followed by no longer being afraid of death. Often, people's lives are drastically changed as a result of a near-death experience, and they lead life more serenely and compassionately. Their belief in God may be deepened, although not necessarily in an orthodox way. Certainly the experience, however interpreted, seems to have a profound effect on the experient and some have claimed to be given psychic powers.

Raymond Moody was not able to draw any positive conclusions from his study, and felt that near-death experiences raised as many questions as answers: 'I am left, not with conclusions or evidence or proofs, but with something less definite – feelings, questions, analogies, puzzling facts to be explained'. There is, as yet, no way of proving which explanation of these experiences is the more convincing. How do we decide if they are hallucinatory or genuinely spiritual? Susan Blackmore (*Dying to Live*, Prometheus Books, 1993) makes three suggestions:

- The explanation must be **coherent** and **specific** – accounting for particular features, not just generalities.

- A theory should not posit extra, or supernatural, realms without good reason.

- The theory should provide testable predictions.

Richard Swinburne (*The Evolution of the Soul,* 1986) argues: 'The principle of credulity might suggest that we ought to take such apparent memories seriously, especially in view of the considerable coincidences between them, as evidence that what subjects thought they had experienced, they really did'. Hugh Montefiore suggests: 'What is at stake is whether … a person is in a conscious or unconscious state … The brain may be functioning … but the person may be completely unconscious as far as the brain is concerned … If so, the conscious experiences of a near-death experience will be mediated not through the brain, but through the soul'.

The problem with the near-death experience is the reliability and verifiability of the testimonies – there is simply the person's word for it and that person may actually be recalling a lost memory of something they had read or heard at some time before.

Parapsychology

Parapsychology is the study of the spiritual realm. Followers of the Spiritualist Movement claim that there is a spirit world where people go after death and that the deceased can be communicated with at séances led by experts known as mediums.

Unfortunately, over the years the Spiritualist Movement has suffered lasting damage to its credibility due to the activities of hoaxers who have used spiritualism to gain money by deliberate deception. Most religious believers

Taking it further...

Interestingly, there is some biblical evidence for spiritualism, when the Witch of Endor raises the spirit of the prophet Samuel (1 Samuel 28:13). Indeed, the Law of Moses expressly forbade the consulting of mediums and ordered their death: 'A man or woman who is a spiritualist or medium among you must be put to death' (Leviticus 20:27).

At a séance, a table levitates so quickly that it appears as a blur in the photo. Note that the medium is in a trance

are naturally cautious about any engagement in parapsychological activities, on the grounds that they are forbidden in scripture, but also because they may be spiritually, emotionally and psychologically dangerous. Many suggest that they may have some value in helping those who are bereaved, but serve no better function than bereavement counselling may do. However, in an age when non-theistic spirituality is very popular, there is a growing interest in and acceptance of beliefs and practices which explore the possibilities of a non-physical world which is both significant and contactable. The range of paranormal services and products which can now be purchased – predictive cards featuring unicorns and angels, readings with mediums and psychics, and a vast range of different alternative therapies, such as reiki and cranio-sacral therapy, which tap into the non-physical aspects of the human personality – suggest that people are spiritually hungry and seek to be fed and reassured in many ways.

Philosophers have also questioned the very purpose of the spirit world – is it just a continuation of life on earth and, if so, then what is the point of it? However, John Hick, though sceptical, argued that spiritualism should not be taken lightly. In *Philosophy of Religion* (Prentice Hall, 1973) he wrote: '… the best cases of trance utterance are impressive and puzzling and taken at face value are indicative of survival and communication after death'.

Reincarnation

'As rivers flow to their rest in the ocean and there leave behind them name and form, so the knower, liberated from name and form, reaches that divine Person beyond the beyond' (Chandogya Upanishad).

Transmigration of souls, also called **reincarnation**, is the rebirth in another body (after physical death) of some critical part of a person's personality or spirit. Within Buddhism, the term rebirth or re-becoming is preferred to reincarnation, as the latter is taken to imply that there is a fixed entity that is reborn. This notion of reincarnation raises questions about the relationship of the soul with the brain and body. The claim is that reincarnated people remember previous lives or even show similar physical marks from their previous life. If that is the case, does the soul affect the brain and give it information, and is the soul able to affect the actual physical body? *Karma* is the principle of cause and effect in Hinduism and Buddhism, which asserts that all acts or deeds leave their influence on a future transmigration of the actor. In other words, the current situation of a human being is the consequence of the person's actions and thoughts in current and past lives.

Within Hinduism, life and death are regarded as part of the cycle of existence. A person lives out their life then, on death, their soul, as the conscious character and memory-bearing self, is reborn again in another body. This cycle goes on through many lives until the soul achieves ultimate reality (*nirvana*) and is united with Brahman. This is known as reincarnation (or 'transmigration of the soul'). The ultimate reality is Brahman and it is union with Brahman that all souls seek. 'Just as a person casts off worn-out garments and puts on others that are new, even so does the disembodied soul cast off worn-out bodies and take on others that are new' (Bhagavad Gita).

Taking it further...

For Hindus, the soul is not the same as a person's conscious self. The fact that humans are psycho-physical beings is an illusion, what John Hick in *Death and Eternal Life* (ibid.) refers to as: '… a temporary expression or organ or instrument of the eternal soul, one indeed of a succession of such expressions which constitute the successive rebirths of that soul'.

The soul's journey from life to life is governed by the notion of *karma* (action), whereby a person's exact reincarnation is determined by how good or bad their *karma* was in the previous life. In the Vedantic tradition, the soul (*jiva*) is eternal and identical to Brahman. However, it dwells in a state of *maya*, which is unreal and finite. The soul exists in a state of illusion and separateness from Brahman.

The soul, in its state of illusion, regards itself as being enclosed in a set of 'bodies' or coverings – the 'gross body' (*sthula sharira*), which is the physical body, and the 'subtle body' (*linga sharira*), which is the mind, the intellect, the emotions and the spiritual aspect of a person. These are the aspects of a person that change and develop in their lifetimes, and the changes are called *samskaras*, or impressions. It is the subtle body that is reincarnated. Hick described it thus: 'The subtle body may accordingly be characterised as a psychic organism consisting of a structure of mental dispositions, but differing from 'person' in that it lacks self-consciousness'.

The soul is not only reincarnated on earth. There are also other realms of existence, some joyful, some painful, where the soul has to face the consequences of the good or bad deeds (*karma*) done on earth. However, these realms do not lead the soul on to *nirvana*. It is only in the physical body on earth that the soul has the freedom and responsibility to act and make decisions for itself, so it is through repeated physical lives on earth that the soul ultimately discovers the path to perfection and enlightenment (*moksha*).

Hindu scholars have argued that the empirical evidence for reincarnation lies in the fact that it explains many odd phenomena in human life – for instance, our fear of death could stem from knowledge gained in previous lives. Likewise, reincarnation could explain why a child may be a 'born genius' such as Mozart. John Hick, however, was not convinced by this argument, claiming that such phenomena may simply be due to instinct and 'exceptionally fortunate genetic combinations'.

Philosophically, reincarnation presents a number of problems. If we accept that the human personality is made up of a combination of physical body, memory and psychological pattern (personal identity), then:

- On reincarnation, bodily continuity is lost.
- If we cannot remember our previous lives, then memory is lost too.
- This leaves only the psychological pattern of personal character remaining.

Evidence for reincarnation

Dr Ian Stevenson, a psychiatrist at the University of Virginia, has researched evidence for reincarnation. Stevenson doesn't use hypnosis; instead, he has investigated a large number of cases in which people claim to have memories of a previous life and where some who knew the person in that life can corroborate these memories. The person sometimes has birthmarks, which seem to substantiate the claims, and generally recognises people and

Taking it further...

In *Karma and Rebirth* (Madras, 1974), Anima Sen Gupta noted: '... when a man dies, his thought-energy in the form of samskaras do not get scattered into space; but this energy remains stored up in the subtle body'.

Taking it further...

In *The Problem of Rebirth*, Sri Aurobindo (Pondicherry, 1972) wrote: 'The true foundation of the theory of rebirth is the evolution of the soul ... out of the veil of matter and its gradual self-finding'.

possessions from the previous life. Although the case for reincarnation, at least in some instances, is quite strongly supported by Stevenson's work, it is not without its difficulties:

- Almost all the cases he describes come from societies in which the reality of reincarnation is accepted, which makes it possible that belief in it may be merely a cultural phenomenon.

- In some cases, there was a long time-gap between the person's first claim to have the memories and Stevenson's investigation, which makes the problems of possible secondary elaboration more difficult to eliminate.

- Because of language difficulties, Stevenson usually had to rely on interpreters, who may have introduced biases of their own into what was said.

All this means that it would be impossible to know if one person is the reincarnation of another. The most it can offer is a vague, unconscious thread of memory linking all the past lives together. In effect, all we can say is that reincarnated people are similar to, rather than the same as, those who went before. Hick, in *Death and Eternal Life* (Westminster, 1994), observed that: 'There can be general similarities of character found in such qualities as selfishness and unselfishness, introverted or extroverted types of personality … but such general similarities would never by themselves lead or entitle us to identify the two as the same person'.

However, this does not invalidate reincarnation as a philosophical concept. Hick suggested that the final proof for the doctrine of reincarnation is the same as he suggested for Christianity, namely eschatological verification – at the end of time, we shall know: '… reincarnation, in some forms, makes sufficient connection with actual or possible human experience to constitute it a factual claim'.

Rebirth

Rebirth is a Buddhist concept that has certain similarities to, but also some important differences from, the Hindu notion of reincarnation. Most important among these is the doctrine of *anatta* ('no soul'). The Buddha taught that everything is composite, that is, temporary and impermanent (*anicca*) and that all existence is therefore unsatisfactory, imperfect and vulnerable to evil (*dukkha*).

Buddhism teaches that a person is made up of the physical body and four mental elements – feeling, perception, moral will and consciousness, which are together called the *nama-rupa* ('name form'). When the physical body dies, the *nama-rupa* is released and the character aspects of the dead person are reborn into the new person, forming his/her non-conscious psychic element – the *vinnana.* Moreover, rebirth may not necessarily be back to earth – there are also said to be many other spiritual worlds and realms.

Everything that changes is impermanent and this includes the physical body. The real self is eternal and unchanging. If it is to be eternal, therefore, the soul must rid itself of all change and achieve *nirvana*, which is the end of

Taking it further...

Many Buddhist believe that the first moment of the new life carries a link from the last moments of the previous life.

rebirth. It does this through the gradual realisation, over a number of lifetimes, of the nature of the ultimate reality. In doing so, the individual may remember aspects of their previous lives – indeed the Buddha himself is said to have recalled thousands of his previous lives. However, although this feels real, ultimately it is not – for there is no soul, no self. John Hick describes rebirth: '… there is no ordinary-language self, but that the mind or self or person is a wholly temporal reality … there is no empirical self or person'.

Rebirth raises many difficult questions. Most significant is the issue of verifiability. If there are rebirths in other worlds and realms, then how can life after death be proven? Moreover, the Buddha taught that rebirths on earth need not be as human beings. In *The Book of Gradual Sayings*, he declared: '… more numerous are those beings who, deceasing as men, are reborn in Purgatory, who are reborn in the wombs of animals, who are reborn in the Realm of Ghosts'.

It is, therefore, questionable whether or not rebirth constitutes life after death in the accepted sense, for so much of it lies outside the earthly sphere of understanding and intelligibility. Much depends on the notion of memory and whether or not the individual really can recall their previous lives. Hick observes: 'It may be that certain psychic formations which were part of the previous individual are now part of him. But if they are not accompanied by memory, can they be said to constitute the same person?'

Karma and rebirth

Before leaving this notion entirely, it is worth understanding how the concept of *karma* comes into issues of rebirth. In the Buddhist theory of *karma*, the word is given a more specific meaning than the usual 'action' and refers to 'volitional action' or 'intentional action', in other words an action that is deliberately willed. This means that Buddhists distinguish between actions that are carried out with no clear intention and actions that are motivated by the wish to achieve a particular goal. Only the latter kind, volitional actions, carry a moral consequence; other actions are morally neutral.

There are two factors that determine whether an action is good or bad. The first is the **intention** behind the action, and the second is the **type of result** it produces. Intention is always the main factor in the Buddhist theory of *karma*, since even the result produced depends on intention. Good actions produce happiness. They arise from generosity, kindness and wisdom and benefit all concerned. Bad actions produce suffering for the person doing the action and are motivated by craving, aggression or ignorance. In determining a *karmic* result, the intention is more important than the action itself. Buddhists claim that *karmic* results affect us either mentally, physically or both and they colour the way we experience the world as well as the way we relate to ourselves.

In general, there are four types of *karmic* effect:

1 the fully-ripened, or maximum, effect of an action
For example, an action motivated by hatred will cause rebirth in the hells.

2 the effect is similar to the cause
For example, if we are often criticised, belittled or lied to by others, this is the result of lying in the past. If we have spoken harsh words in the past,

everything that is said to us seems offensive or insulting, and whatever we say provokes an argument.

3 the conditioning effect; it acts on our environment
For example, stealing may cause rebirth in areas stricken by famine.

4 the proliferation effect
This refers to the way in which an action done before will tend to be repeated again and again. It will become a habit.

A *karmic* result might be immediate, or it might come in the medium term or the long term. *Karmic* effects can come either in this present life or in the next life or in later future lives. The law of *karma* is seen as a natural law inherent in the nature of things. *Karma* is not operated by God or any other supreme being, because for Buddhists natural laws do not require any supernatural intervention in order to function. Good actions produce good results and bad actions produce bad results naturally, without any outside intervention. This means that the results of *karma* are not described by Buddhists as forms of 'reward' or 'punishment', because the idea of reward and punishment depends on a belief in a supreme power sitting in judgement on us and sharing out good and bad experiences in accordance with that judgement. In Buddhism, there is nobody to judge us, there is nobody to decide our future. We determine our future by the way we act and the way we think. We have nobody to blame but ourselves for any unfortunate *karmic* results that we may suffer.

Resurrection of the body

'The resurrection of Jesus is a … disclosure of the ultimate nature of reality as spiritual, and of the final unity of the material universe as the perfected unity of all things in God' (Keith Ward, *Christianity: A Guide for the Perplexed*, SPCK Publishing, 2007).

Bodily resurrection is an important concept in monotheistic traditions and is a central doctrine of Christianity. It is based on the notion that, at some future date (sometimes called Judgement Day), God, through an act of divine love, will restore the dead to eternal life in bodily form. It is not the resuscitation of corpses, but the re-creation by God of the human individual, not as the physical being which has died, but as a spiritual being. Jesus Christ said: 'I am the resurrection and the life. He who believes in me, though he die, yet shall he live' (John 11:25). This message was starkly demonstrated in Christ's own resurrection from death, where he appeared before his disciples with a physical body: 'Look at my hands and my feet … touch me and see; a ghost does not have flesh and bones as you see I have' (Luke 24:39). There is further support for the view that mind and body must be united in the resurrection in Job 19:25: 'After my skin has been destroyed, then in my flesh shall I see God'.

The resurrected person is not the same as the one who died. He or she will have a spiritual body (*soma pneumatikon*), rather than a flesh and blood one, which contains all of their memories and characteristics and which will endure forever: 'For the trumpet will sound, the dead will be raised imperishable, and we shall be changed. For the perishable must clothe itself with the imperishable, and the mortal with immortality' (1 Corinthians

The resurrection of Jesus

Taking it further...

The apostle Paul wrote that, when a person dies, they are extinct. They are, in effect, annihilated by death. God, through an act of divine love and sovereign power at the time of judgement, resurrects (or re-creates) the dead.

15:52). This, observed Keith Ward, was a logical consequence of post-mortem existence: 'But for those who think there is a God, a spiritual reality that is the cause of the whole physical universe, it will seem obvious that there is a spiritual realm as well as a physical realm' (*God: A Guide for the Perplexed*, Oneworld Publications, 2002).

Thomas Aquinas believed that eternal life required a body and a soul. In *Summa Theologica*, he wrote: 'Now that the soul is what makes our body live; so the soul is the primary source of all these activities that differentiate levels of life: growth, sensation, movement, understanding mind or soul, it is the form of our body … the natural condition of the soul is to be united to the body ... it has a natural desire for union with the body, hence the will cannot be perfectly at rest until the soul is again joined to a body. When this takes place, man rises from the dead.' Aquinas believed that the soul animated the body and gave it life. He called the soul the *anima*.

Questions surrounding bodily resurrection

The notion of bodily resurrection raises many philosophical questions. Of greatest concern is the issue of whether a resurrected body is really 'us' or simply a copy of us. If we have truly died then, by definition, we cannot be brought back to life. Is resurrection therefore concerned with copies and clones?

Questions also arise over the age and appearance of the resurrected body. Is the body resurrected in perfect condition, with physical defects and illnesses cured, or do the sick and handicapped remain so for eternity? The only evidence we have is the resurrection of Jesus himself. Even his disciples did not recognise him at first, and he seemed to have the ability to go through locked doors and to appear at will. He still bore the scars of crucifixion, although the wounds appear to have healed. This prompted Bertrand Russell to speculate that, perhaps: 'The continuity of a human body is a matter of appearance and behaviour, not of substance'.

John Hick attempted to answer this question with his **Replica Theory**. He suggested that, if someone died and appeared in another place with the same memories and physical features, then it would be meaningful to regard this replica as the same person because they would be conscious of being the same person as the one who had earlier died. He argued that an all-powerful God would be able to create a replica of a dead person, complete with all the individual's memories and characteristics and to place him or her in a world inhabited by resurrected persons. In *Philosophy of Religion*, he said that life after death could be: '… as a resurrection replica in a different world altogether, a resurrection world inhabited only by resurrected persons'.

There are several problems with this theory. Firstly, if God can make one replica, then he could make multiple replicas, which surely undermine personal identity. Furthermore, the concept of a replica is questionable, since we are aware that a replica is usually not considered to be as valuable as the original. As far as Hick's scenarios are concerned, he asks us to envisage Person A being transported from one place to another without crossing time and space, or being raised to life on the other side of the Atlantic. Such scenarios are counter-intuitive and Hicks even goes on to

Taking it further...

T.S. Boase, in *Death in the Middle Ages* (McGraw Hill, 1972), noted the curious fact that, in many medieval Christian books about death, the resurrected dead, regardless of the age they died, would be the same age as Christ on his death, namely 'thirty-two years and three months'.

Taking it further...

Interestingly, this finds support in the Bible. In the Book of Revelation, it describes the resurrection thus: 'Then I saw a new heaven and a new earth, for the first heaven and the first earth had passed away ... I saw the Holy City, the new Jerusalem, coming down out of heaven from God' (Revelation 21:1-2).

Taking it further...

Hick explained the principle of **eschatological verification** by using the analogy of two people walking down a road, one believing that it leads to the celestial city, and one believing that there is no final destination. They will not know which one is right until they reach the end of the road. Then, at last, the truth will be known.

suggest that we are not expected to believe that they *would* happen, but rather that, if there were no other good explanation for it, then we would be compelled to accept what had happened. He adds a further scenario, suggesting that Person A is resurrected in a place inhabited by resurrected bodies. In some ways this is more conceivable, since it does not demand that we envisage what seems to be physically possible in *this* world; rather, that it is occurring in a world beyond our experience, in which, conceivably, anything would happen.

The problem remains, however, that if bodily resurrection does not take place until the end of time, how can life after death be verified now? Hick's solution was the principle of 'eschatological verification'. He argued that, though we may not be able to verify post-mortem existence in our earthly lives, one day, at the end of time, if there is life after death, we will know.

For theists, for the body to be raised after death demands the direct intervention of God, and is more consistent with the biblical teaching that man is soul and body, but that without God's power and love, man cannot survive the death of the physical body. As God raised Jesus from the dead, he will raise all those who die and who will then face his judgement. The joys of the after life for most theistic believers, but especially for Christians, are by no means automatic. Rather, they are reserved for those who have made a commitment of faith. Without God, the after life is meaningless, or worse.

Immortality of the soul

Despite the importance of the body as a creation of God, in the monotheistic traditions of Christianity, Islam and Judaism, scholars have argued that the physical body cannot live without the soul – which is the real self and is non-physical, mental, and spiritual. The body is contingent and will decay and die, but the soul is non-contingent and cannot die. Thus, when the body dies, the soul continues to live. In *Range of Reason* (Bles, 1953), Maritain said: 'A spiritual soul cannot be corrupted, since it possesses no physical matter ... the human soul cannot die. Once it exists, it cannot disappear; it will necessarily exist for ever'.

Plato

Plato believed that the body belongs to the physical world and, like all physical things, will one day cease to exist. The soul, however, belongs to a higher realm where eternal truths, such as justice, love and goodness, endure forever. He argued that the soul seeks to free itself from the physical world and go to the higher realm of true reality (the realm of the Forms), where it will be able to spend eternity contemplating truth, beauty and goodness. In *Phaedo*, Plato wrote of Socrates' death: '... when I have drunk the poison, I shall leave you and go to the joys of the blessed'.

Plato put forward two famous arguments for dualism. In his dialogue the *Meno*, Plato has Socrates get a slave boy do some simple geometry and reach conclusions which the boy could not have learnt in this life (as a rough equivalent, imagine doing a difficult multiplication sum – you will come up with an answer you have never learnt before, and even if you do a simple multiplication sum correctly, the question remains of how you *know* it is the right answer). Through Socrates, Plato draws the conclusion that the geometrical knowledge must have come down in the boy's soul when it descended from the eternally-real world to join his body to make a human being. Our soul forgets its heavenly knowledge in its descent to earth and education is needed to enable it to remember. This idea is called Plato's 'Doctrine of Recollection'.

Plato's second argument is in the *Phaedo*, and is based on his concept that 'like gives rise to like'. If this is the case, then it follows that body and mind are so different that it is impossible that body could be made out of mind and mind made out of body. The body is made up of bits of the material world and the soul 'made' of an invisible, intellectual and immaterial (non-physical) reality. It is in the material world that change, decay and death are possible, so the soul must be an eternal reality which existed before birth and will continue to exist after the death of the body.

Plato's ideas about the soul have long been discredited as far as philosophy is concerned. They depend on a certain view of the relationship of mind and body, and empirical investigation has replaced Plato's abstract reasoning about them. In other words, we use psychology to find out what Plato believed we could know just by thinking.

René Descartes

Descartes, sceptical of the physical world, which could be a source of constant deception under the agency of a malign demon, rejected it as a source of certainty. Rather, certainty was to be found in the thinking processes which led one to doubt the material world. Such a view leads necessarily to the view that the soul, the unseen, immaterial part of human identity, must be the only possible meaningful way of understanding an after life.

Immanuel Kant

For Kant, the purpose of existence was to achieve the *summum bonum* or complete good. He argued that human beings could not achieve this in one lifetime and that God was, therefore, morally obliged to help humanity to achieve the complete good by granting us eternal life. Otherwise, he said, morality would be pointless. In *Critique of Pure Reason* (Cambridge University Press, 1999 ed.), he wrote: 'The *summum bonum* is only possible on the presupposition of the immortality of the soul'.

What has concerned scholars and theologians most over the centuries has been the question of where the soul goes when the physical body dies. The traditional Christian view has been that if a dying person has asked for, and received, God's forgiveness for their sins, they are said to die in a 'state of grace' and will go to Heaven. However, those who do not die in such a state will go either to Hell, a place of eternal punishment where the worst sinners go, or Purgatory, a place where lapsed believers go to be punished and then purified from sin.

Modern scholars have challenged these notions in recent years. In *The God Delusion* (Bantam, 2006), Richard Dawkins scathingly describes Purgatory as '... a Hadean waiting room where dead souls go if their sins aren't bad enough to send them to Hell'. At the same time, John Hick regards the notion of Hell as: '... horrible and disturbing beyond words; and the thought

Immanuel Kant

Taking it further...

Kant's view about the purpose of existence was supported by John Hick in *Death and Eternal Life*. He said that without eternal life, there was little point in morality: 'If the human potential is to be fulfilled in the lives of individuals, these lives must be prolonged far beyond the limits of our present bodily existence'.

of such torment being deliberately inflicted by divine decree is totally incompatible with the idea of God as infinite love'.

Heaven is also problematic, since it is unclear exactly what it is. Monotheistic religions have tended to describe it as a place of paradise, without pain or sorrow, where those who have loved God dwell with him forever. This creates the problem of what actually happens there – can there be a worthwhile human existence where there are no challenges and purposes? Aquinas himself regarded heaven as a beatific vision (*viseo dei*) which is a state of highest joy – the unchanging vision of God: '… we must not, therefore, imagine God in the beatific vision as some outside object to look at, but as dwelling within the very essence of our soul …' (*Summa Theologica*).

In *The Tragic Sense of Life* (Fontana, 1972), Miguel de Unamuno refined this notion, suggesting that humans live forever not in physical form, but in the memory of God: 'After I have died, God will go on remembering me, and to be remembered by God, to have my consciousness sustained by the Supreme Consciousness, is not that, perhaps, to be?'

However, the notion of an immortal soul has difficulties of its own. Most notable among them would be the question of how the soul, without a physical body, would relate to its surroundings and to other souls. In *Survival and the Idea of Another World* (SPR, 1953), H. H. Price argued that any experiences that the soul has in a post-mortem experience would be 'mind dependent'. By this he meant that what the soul perceived would be formed out of the mental images it acquired in life. In a sense, the soul would perceive things in a physical way because that is what it was used to. He suggests that this new world will require souls to communicate with other souls by some sort of telepathy or extra-sensory perception and that the world itself will be fashioned by the power of our own desires and the desires of those around us – because there is no physical body, then the soul is forced to supply its own; a dream body for a dream world: '… the 'stuff' or 'material' of such a world would come in the end from one's memories, and the 'form' of it from one's desires'.

However, one has to question whether or not this would really be life after death. The individual will continue to exist, but will not have proper interaction with other people and, if everything stems from his/her own desires, then he/she will not have any new experiences, nor the opportunity to develop to full potential, as John Hick observes: 'Instead of a world that is given to us and to which we must adapt ourselves, we shall inhabit a world created by our own minds and expressing our own desires. Could such a world continue the person-making process begun on earth?'

Which is most convincing?

To assess which is a more convincing view of the after life depends very powerfully on the religious and cultural background from which a person comes and on whether they think it is meaningful to talk of life after death at all. When examined, none emerges as independently more convincing than the other. Perhaps the answer lies in thinking of life after death as anti-realist, rather than envisaging it as a real, physical mode of being. In other words, those who take these views do not believe that 'life after death' can be known in terms of being a future reality that we can experience, but they still think it can be shown that the statement 'I believe in life after death' is in some sense true and worth making.

Taking it further...

More radically still, Charles Hartshorne in *The Logic of Perfection* (Opencourt, 1962), argued in favour of what he called 'social immortality', that is, we live on, not physically, but in the ways in which we have influenced the lives of those who come after us and in the eternal memory of God: '… the true immortality is everlasting fame before God'.

Taking it further...

This would be more like a post-mortem dream than eternal life. It could even be a nightmare, as H. H. Price points out: 'Each man's purgatory would be just the automatic consequence of his own desires'.

The thinking of Ludwig Wittgenstein is helpful here. He observed:

> *Suppose, for instance, we knew people who foresaw the future: make forecasts for years and years ahead; and they described some sort of Judgement Day. Queerly enough, even if there were such a thing, and even if it were more convincing than I have described … belief in this happening would not be a religious belief.*

(*Lectures and Conversations on Aesthetics, Psychology and Religious Beliefs* cited in *Wittgenstein and Philosophy of Religion* ed. by Robert L. Arrington and Mark Addis, Routledge, 2001).

Wittgenstein is suggesting that, if the Last Judgement is just another possible future event for which we may or may not have evidence, then it loses its religious significance. It is only when the belief exists within the complex natural setting of a web of religious practice that it has a meaning. Take it out of this living context and then it is no longer a real belief and to discuss its 'truth' as if it were just another fact which may or may not be true is to completely misunderstand the nature and use of religious language.

The Last Judgement, *detail of a fresco by Giotto*

Another non-realist approach to life after death sees it as a myth or symbol. In this view, talk of heaven is really talk about the happiness of someone in this life who lives an unselfish and generous life. Talk of hell is really talk about the misery of the selfish egoist in this life and to speak of the 'Last Judgement' symbolises our deepest motivation for what we do. Some Liberal Jews and Christians have adopted this wholly symbolic way of thinking about life after death. They have done this either simply because they think that in our modern world belief in a realist, literal life after death is no longer possible for many people or because they consider that realist beliefs about life after death confuse and disguise the true religious message, which is that what matters most of all is the sort of person you are and the sort of person you are becoming. This view is akin to the process of demythologising which was proposed by Rudolph Bultmann in the 1920s.

This view is, of course, quite unsatisfactory for those who believe that there are important implications for life after death in terms of rewards and punishments. Nevertheless, in an age when the need for empirical evidence is, for some, the stumbling block of religious belief, then it has its appeal.

2.2 Religious language

Key Ideas

- ☐ **What is religious language?**

- ☐ **The verification and falsification debate**

- ☐ **The *via negativa***

- ☐ **How religious language is used: cognitive and non-cognitive language**

- ☐ **Language game theory: a postmodern view**

What is religious language?

Religious language is concerned with speaking about God. It is the way people speak about what they believe and why they believe it and it encompasses worship, practice, morality, dogma and doctrine. Religious language includes words that are:

- unique in the description of God, such as 'omnipotent'

- descriptions of religious belief, such as the Second Coming or the Last Judgement

- religious technical terms, such as 'sin' or 'grace'

- everyday terms that are given a religious meaning, such as 'love' and 'goodness'.

Religious language is difficult because our words are not adequate to speak about a transcendent God who is above and beyond all human experience. We want to speak about God but we do not have the words to do so properly. Throughout the ages, scholars have attempted to find ways of making human language work effectively when applied to God, but this has been very difficult to do – it has often resulted in misunderstandings, obscurity and confusion, leading some scholars to suggest that it may be impossible to speak about God at all. What follows is an examination of the main approaches taken by scholars in their attempts to make religious language meaningful.

Cognitive and non-cognitive language

Religious language can be cognitive or non-cognitive.

- **Cognitive** (or **realist**) language deals with factual statements that can be proved to be either true or false. These can be either empirically provable, such as 'The Queen is the Head of State', or statements that, as far as believers are concerned, contain meaningful factual content, such as 'God exists' or 'God loves me'. In *Theology and Falsification*

Taking it further...

There have been particular problems in speaking of God 'doing' something in the world – creating, sustaining, or intervening. Similar issues arise when speaking of how God displays qualities such as mercy, justice or love. These problems arise from the belief that God's nature means that he is outside the world, and yet he acts within it to maintain a relationship with his people.

(SCM, 1955), Anthony Flew described cognitive language as consisting of: '…crypto-commands, expressions of wishes, disguised ejaculations, concealed ethics, or anything else but assertions'.

- **Non-cognitive** (or **anti-realist***) language deals with statements that are not to be taken factually, but are to be understood in other ways – for example as symbols, metaphors, myths or moral commands. These are statements that express a religious truth within the religious community in which it belongs – for example, 'Jesus is the Lamb of God' is a truth for Christians, but may not be even meaningful to someone outside that community. In other words, there is no objective universal truth – the truth or falsity of a statement depends upon its context.

The verification and falsification debate

Can religious language ever be meaningful? Some argue that it is not because it does not deal with factually verifiable assertions. Others claim that it is meaningful because it can be verified, at least to the believer's satisfaction. The verification and falsification debate is, therefore, crucial to an understanding of religious language.

The verification principle

The verification principle stemmed from the movement known as **Logical Positivism** and, in particular, from a group of philosophers in the 1920s known as the **Vienna Circle**. They applied the principles of science and mathematics to language and argued that, like knowledge, language had to be based on experience. For a statement to be considered meaningful it had to be verifiable by our sense experiences – touch, smell, taste, hearing or sight. This is the basis of empirical testing. A statement must meet one or more of the following criteria to be deemed to be meaningful:

- **Analytic statements**
  These are true by definition (for example, 'A circle is round'). These are *a priori* statements that are true because they contain their own verification. Thus, 'A spinster is an unmarried woman' is necessarily true because by definition a spinster is unmarried.

- **Mathematical statements**
  A. J. Ayer observed that apparent inconsistencies in mathematical calculations would be discovered to be the product of human error rather than a genuine difference in the facts of the case. For example, if 5+5 were suddenly found to equal 9, a recalculation would quickly demonstrate that an error of addition had been made.

- **Synthetic statements**
  These are statements that can be verified or falsified by subjecting them to empirical testing. They are *a posteriori* statements which cover claims that can be verified or falsified through observation and are therefore contingently true or false. For instance, 'Dogs bark' is verifiably true in the same way that 'All swans are green' can be proved to be false. Both statements are, therefore, meaningful. Theoretical statements such as 'There is life on other planets' are also meaningful, since they may be verified or falsified at some time in the future – we know the means of

Taking it further...

Cognitive claims are sometimes referred to in the **correspondence theory of truth,** which highlights a direct link between the language used and the concepts or objects to which that language refers, usually by means of some empirical observation. Non-cognitive claims are sometimes referred to in the **coherence theory of truth**, whereby a statement is true if it fits in (coheres) with other truth claims.

their verification even if it has not yet been possible to carry it out. However, a statement such as 'Love of money is the root of all evil' is not meaningful since it is impossible to verify.

The Vienna Circle concluded that religious statements were meaningless, on the basis that they do not satisfy any of these criteria, because religious language claims are subjective and cannot therefore be empirically tested and verified. In *Language, Truth and Logic* (Penguin, 1936), A. J. Ayer observed that, since the existence of God cannot be rationally demonstrated, it is not even probable, since the term 'god' is a metaphysical term referring to a transcendent being which cannot therefore have any literal significance. Interestingly, he observed that the same had therefore to be the case for atheistic and agnostic statements, since *any* statement which includes the term 'god' is meaningless. Ayer argued that, since claims about God's existence cannot be contradicted, they are not 'significant propositions' – they are neither true nor false, but cannot be valid: 'The notion of a being whose essential attributes are non-empirical is not an intelligible notion at all'.

Ayer was not simply concerned with talking about God, but also with all other religious language, including talk of an after life, which cannot be verified either. Talk of a soul he dismissed as meaningless since it is a metaphysical assertion to say that 'there is something imperceptible inside a man, which is his soul or his real self, and that it goes on living after he is dead'.

Talk of religious experience was also soundly dismissed by Ayer as being talk of experience which cannot be validated empirically: 'The fact that people have religious experiences is interesting from the psychological point of view, but it does not in any way imply that there is such a thing as religious knowledge.'

Criticisms of the verification principle

Critics of the verification principle say it is flawed because it deems as meaningless many statements that are, clearly, meaningful. For example:

- Statements that express **unverifiable opinions or emotions**, such as 'I love you', are deemed to be meaningless. Although we may not be able to define precisely what it means to love another person, when we make the claim it is understood as meaningful; hence it is at least meaningful in principle.

- **Ethical and moral** statements such as 'Do not kill' are regarded as meaningless. Nevertheless, it has been possible to establish both secular and religious laws based on such claims, at least some of which are considered for the most part to be universalisable.

- The **laws of science** cannot be absolutely verified. For example, the sentence 'Gravity always makes a thing fall to the ground' is untestable and therefore said to be meaningless.

- **Historical** statements such as 'The Battle of Waterloo took place in 1815' are regarded as meaningless because they cannot be verified by sense experience – there is no one alive who could claim to have experienced it.

- The verification principle itself cannot be verified, for there is no sense experience that can prove it to be true.

A. J. Ayer, in 1959

Taking it further...

The Vienna Circle was heavily influenced by Ludwig Wittgenstein's **picture theory of language**, which said that a statement is meaningful if it can be defined, or pictured, in the real world.

Taking it further...

Bryan McGee, in *Confessions of a Philosopher* (Phoenix, 1997), observed: 'People began to realise that this glittering new scalpel was, in one operation after another, killing the patient'.

To address these criticisms, in *Language, Truth and Logic* (Penguin, 1936), A. J. Ayer proposed a 'strong' and 'weak' form of the verification principle. A strong verification occurs when there is no doubt that a statement is true, such as 'The Pope is a Catholic'. Weak verification occurs where there is not absolute certainty, but where there is a strong likelihood of truth because of the evidence, such as 'Nelson won the Battle of Trafalgar'. Ayer wrote: 'A proposition is verifiable in the strong sense if, and only if, its truth could be conclusively established... but it is verifiable in the weak sense if it is possible for experience to render it probable'.

The problem still remained, however, that religious language statements are unverifiable because they refer to a transcendent being which is not, itself, even verifiable in principle. Yet Keith Ward, in *Holding Fast to God* (One World, 1982), observed that God's existence *could* be verified in principle since 'If I were God I would be able to check the truth of my own existence'. Moreover, John Hick (*Faith and Knowledge*, Palgrave Macmillan, 1988) asserted that, since many religious language claims are historical, then if other historical statements are allowed because they are verifiable in principle, it follows that statements such as 'Jesus rose from the dead on Easter Sunday' would also have to be permitted as meaningful since it is, in principle, verifiable.

> ## Taking it further...
>
> Ayer claimed that, if it was possible to know what would, in principle, verify a statement, then that statement would be meaningful. However, this does not really help, because in theory virtually any statement could be verifiable if it is possible to say what would, in principle, serve as the means of its verification.

> ## Taking it further...
>
> John Hick illustrated this in his *Parable of the Celestial City*. In this story, two people are walking along the only road. One believes that it leads to the Celestial City. The other believes that it is a road to nowhere. They have many trials and adventures as they travel. One interprets them as being sent by God to prepare them for life in the Celestial City; the other sees them as random chance. Only when they reach the end of the road will they know the truth. This is **eschatological verification**. However, although it is impossible to verify the destination whilst on the road, the journey and their beliefs as to where it is heading, are still meaningful for the travellers.

The falsification principle

The falsification principle is concerned not with what makes something true, but with what would, in principle, make it false. John Hick, in *Faith and Knowledge* (Collins, 1978), observed: 'In order to say something which may possibly be true, we must say something which may possibly be false'. Anthony Flew claimed that religious statements are meaningless because there is nothing that can count against them. He argued that religious believers are so convinced of the truth of their religious statements that they often refuse to consider evidence suggesting that God does not exist. As a result, religious language 'dies the death of a thousand qualifications' (*The Existence of God*, ed. John Hick, Macmillan, 1964). For example, he claimed, believers say God is all-loving and all-powerful and continue to believe this despite the evidence of great suffering in the world which, he suggested, they choose to ignore. He asks of religious believers, 'What would have to occur or to have occurred to constitute for you a disproof of the love of, or the existence of, God?' Effectively, Flew argues that if nothing is allowed to count against a claim such as 'God loves us as a father loves his children', then the claim means nothing, since *anything* is apparently consistent with the claim, even the death of thousands of children in an earthquake.

Does a gardener tend this spot?

By way of example, Flew used John Wisdom's famous *Parable of the Gardener* to highlight how believers continue to refuse to accept anything that counts against the existence of God. In this story, two men are in an overgrown garden. The first man sees some plants growing among the weeds and suggests that there must be a gardener. But none of the neighbours has ever seen a gardener there. So the first man says that the gardener must come at night. The second man argues that if there was a gardener then he would have removed the weeds. The first man replies that the garden has a design about it, and he suggests that the gardener must be invisible. The men examine the garden and find some things that suggest a gardener, and others that do not. Finally, after both have seen all the evidence, the first continues to insist that there is a gardener, but one which is invisible, intangible and inaudible. The second asks what is the difference between such a gardener, and no gardener at all?

Flew argued that religious believers have similarly avoided the evidence by hiding behind phrases such as 'God moves in mysterious ways' rather than considering the empirical evidence. He said that for believers to claim that 'God exists' means that they must also be open to the evidence that God may not exist. However, Flew felt that believers were reluctant to do so and, consequently, the religious language they used was meaningless, for it was not falsifiable: 'Now it often seems to people who are not religious as if there was no conceivable event ... the occurrence of which would be admitted by sophisticated religious people to be a sufficient reason for conceding ... "God does not really love us then".'

Alternatives to the falsification principle

However, some scholars have felt that Flew's arguments are a little too extreme and have offered alternative viewpoints:

R. M. Hare introduced the notion of a **blik**. He claimed that when believers use religious language, they are using it in a unique way. 'Bliks', he said, were: 'ways of regarding the world which are in principle neither verifiable nor falsifiable – but modes of cognition to which the terms 'veridical' or 'illusory' properly apply'.

In other words, the believer uses religious language to express concepts that are important to him/her. They make a significant difference to that person's life, which can be empirically observed, and therefore their statements do have meaning. Peter Vardy observed: 'Religious language, therefore, calls people out beyond the frontiers of their existing morality to a different way of living life...' (cited in Cole, 1999).

Basil Mitchell, in the *Parable of the Partisan and the Stranger,* highlighted the fact that many religious believers do accept that their beliefs can be questioned but that, nevertheless, they will continue to believe them even in the face of evidence to the contrary. Mitchell called such beliefs 'significant articles of faith', which the believer accepts to be open to serious challenge but which, in the light of his/her personal experience, he/she will not allow to falsify their belief. This is non-propositional faith – faith rooted in a relationship rather than simply accepting facts about God. Mitchell observed that there are three ways in which the believer can react when their assertions are challenged.

They can treat them as:

- provisional hypotheses to be discarded if experience tells against them

- vacuous formulae, to which experience makes no difference and which make no difference to life

- significant articles of faith, which 'face the full force of the conflict' and may be seriously challenged, but which are not easily abandoned.

Richard Swinburne, in *The Coherence of Theism* (Clarenden, 1977), uses an interesting example to support his view that many such statements still have real meaning:

> *... there are plenty of examples of statements which some people judge to be factual which are not apparently confirmable or disconfirmable through observation. For example: Some of the toys which to all appearances stay in the toy cupboard while people are asleep and no one is watching, actually get up and dance in the middle of the night and then go back to the cupboard, leaving no traces of their activity.'*

R. B. Braithwaite argued that religious language is about the way in which people should behave towards one another and that, therefore, religious claims are meaningful because they express an intention to follow a certain code of behaviour.

The *via negativa*

Language is rich and dynamic – it can express truth and it can express falsehoods. However, how can we know whether a religious statement is expressing truth? One way of doing this, which dates back to ancient times, is through the *via negativa*. This is a theory which suggests that the truth about God can be discovered by speaking negatively about him. It was used by Dionysius in *Mystical Theology*, where he argued that the way to find out what God is like is first to discover what he is *not* like. By ruling out what he is not, we will discover what he is. This is the principle of negation.

Supporters of the principle claim that it avoids the pitfalls of using inadequate human language to describe the qualities of God – it is easier to say what he is not. Peter Cole, in *Philosophy of Religion* (Hodder, 1999), wrote: '... by denying all descriptions of God, you get insight and experience of God rather than unbelief and scepticism'.

Criticisms of the *via negativa*

- Such an approach means that we cannot describe God in factual terms, because it means reducing the divinity of God to the level of human language. Instead of saying 'God is love', we would have to say 'God is not-love', because he is so much more than this term can convey. Since the concept of God as not-love is not rational, it can be argued that the *via negativa* makes speaking of God even more problematic.

Taking it further...

In the *Parable of the Partisan and the Stranger*, a partisan meets a stranger whom he believes is the secret leader of the resistance movement. At times, the stranger seems to be working against the movement, but the partisan is told that it is all part of the stranger's plan. The partisan continues to believe the stranger because he has faith in him, even though his friends find it incomprehensible. However, the partisan's initial meeting with the stranger has been decisive and is the basis on which he is able to continue to hold fast to his belief even when the evidence is ambiguous.

Taking it further...

Some see the *via negativa* as a mystical practice. It begins by negating the least appropriate characterisations of God and then proceeds to negate even the most honorable names for God, until the negation can go no further. What is left, is God.

Taking it further...

Aquinas argued that negation does emphasise the unknowability of God. Moreover, to talk positively about something requires a subject and Aquinas observed that God, who is above all things, and existentially different from them, cannot be a subject.

- The *via negativa* cannot distinguish theism from atheism, since to say that God can only be spoken of in negatives means denying the existence of God altogether.

- Believers always want to speak positively about God and insist that speaking of him in terms of negation fails to say anything meaningful about him at all.

How is religious language used?

Other scholars down the centuries have looked at the ways in which words are used in religious language. Words are not always to be taken literally and the meaning of statements can often depend on an understanding of the way in which religious terms are used. There are several possibilities:

1 Univocal language

Univocal language is about using words in their everyday sense. In religious terms, that means, for example, using 'God's love' and 'Jane's love' to mean the same thing. This way of using language makes it possible to understand God because, in our example, we know the nature of God's love because we understand human love. As Hume observed: 'Wisdom, thought, design, knowledge – these we justly ascribe to him because those words are honourable among men, and we have no other language by which we can express our adoration of him' (*Dialogues Concerning Natural Religion*, Oxford World Classics, ed. 2005).

However, univocal language causes problems of **anthropomorphism** – if we refer to God and humans in the same way, then we are unable to differentiate between them. Aquinas wrote in the *Summa Theologica*: 'But no name belongs to God in the same sense that it belongs to creatures; for instance, wisdom in creatures is a quality, but not in God'.

2 Equivocal language

Equivocal language means that the same word is used with a totally different meaning, or in a vague or ambiguous way. In terms of God, this means using everyday words but, because the nature of God is so different from the nature of humanity, when we refer to God as being 'good' or 'just' we are using the terms in a different way. God's love is not of the same nature and quality as Jane's love. Using equivocal language we can stress the distinctiveness of God's qualities and avoid the problems of anthropomorphism.

However, the problem with equivocal language is that it makes God so different that it becomes difficult, if not impossible, to understand him. Aquinas observed: 'Neither, on the other hand, are names applied to God and creatures in a purely equivocal sense, as some have said. Because if that were so, it follows that from creatures nothing could be known or demonstrated about God at all; for the reasoning would always be exposed to the fallacy of equivocation'.

3 Analogical language (analogy)

Religious language can also be **analogical**. Analogy is a compromise and offers a way of resolving the problems caused by univocal and equivocal language and seeks to enable people to speak meaningfully about the transcendent God. In *A Dictionary of Biblical Interpretation* (SCM Press), Burrell wrote: 'Analogies are proportional similarities which also acknowledge dissimilar features'.

It was Aquinas who first argued that religious language is neither univocal nor equivocal. God, he said, is not a being like other beings, but we can reason about him by using words in a non-literal way that show there is a relationship between a word used in one sense as opposed to another. Analogical language is a means by which we may be compared to God in order to describe God's nature. It uses human terms such as 'good' and 'love' and applies them in a similar, but not identical way to God. Thus, God's love is similar to Jane's but infinitely superior.

Aquinas called this the 'gradation to be found in things'. He said that all the goodness and love in humanity came first from God and, therefore, God and humanity are 'analogously related' to him. All the positive qualities of humanity belong to God in greater and more perfect ways. We understand God through our experience of these human qualities: 'Among beings there are some more and some less good, true, noble and the like... Therefore, there must also be something which is to all beings the cause of their being, goodness, and every other perfection, and this we call God'. Since God is the cause of good things in humanity, we can use the description 'good' of both God and humans but, as the cause of human goodness, God's goodness is greater.

There are two types of analogy:

- **Analogy of proportionality**
  This is the view that all good qualities belong infinitely to God and, in proportion, to humans – for instance, a plant has life, a human has life, God has life; there is a proportionate relationship. In this way, although we cannot fully understand God, we can at least begin to understand his nature.

- **Analogy of attribution**
  This is the view that God is the cause of all good things in humans; therefore, God's attributes are simply a higher level of our own. John Hick offered the examples of 'upwards' analogy, for instance speaking of a dog's faithfulness and then going upwards to human faith in God. In the same way, 'downwards' analogy uses the attributes of God, such as wisdom, and reflects them downwards, so that human wisdom is seen as a pale reflection of God's wisdom.

More recently, Ian Ramsey offered a **models and qualifiers** approach to analogy. A model is an analogy that helps us to express something about God, such as 'God is good'. The model is the word 'good'. We know what good means in human terms and when we apply it to God, it gives us a model to understand the goodness of God. In the same way, we can adapt or

Taking it further...

Analogy works by using human experience. There is a relationship between God and humanity and God makes himself known to humanity through experience – we love one another and, as a result of this experience, understand something of the nature of God's infinite love. In *Philosophy and the Christian Faith* (InterVarsity Press, 1968), Colin Brown noted: 'Divine truth has to be refracted and expressed in terms of human words and finite images'.

'qualify' the model to improve our understanding by putting God's attributes on a greater level, for instance by adding the qualifier that 'God is *infinitely* good'. In this way, we can think of God's goodness in a deeper and more meaningful way.

4 Symbolic language

Religious language can be **symbolic**. A symbol is something that **identifies** a concept that it is referring to and also **participates** in the meaning of that concept. Erika Dinkler-von Schubert, in *A Handbook of Christian Theology*, (Fontana, 1960), defined a symbol as: 'a pattern or object which points to an invisible metaphysical reality and participates in it'. The difference between a symbol and a sign is that the latter simply provides information, such as a street sign. Symbols go beyond that to express what the believer feels about what that symbol conveys.

Symbols may be pictures, objects, actions or words. For example, the national flag is a symbol that conveys patriotism and national identity; the exchange of rings at a wedding symbolises eternal love. Symbols have a special significance in most religious traditions. Thus, the cross in Christianity identifies the religion and also participates in the important Christian concept of the death and resurrection of Jesus Christ, signifying salvation, sacrifice and hope.

Symbolic language, including metaphors, similes, signs and myths, is always non-cognitive language. In religious terms, symbolic statements include Jesus's famous sayings 'I am the light of the world' and 'I am the true vine' or the images used by the Psalmist: 'The Lord is my shepherd' or 'God is my fortress and my high tower'.

Symbols should not be interpreted literally because they are subtle modes of communication about that which is beyond the factual and objective. For this reason, symbols are important in religious language because they are non-cognitive and go beyond our normal understanding.

In support of symbolic language, Paul Tillich in *Systematic Theology* (Nisbet, 1951) claimed that it was a positive way of expressing the nature of God in terms of 'the ground of our being', or 'that which concerns us ultimately'. In *Dynamics of Faith* (Harper, 1958), he commented: 'Symbolic language alone is able to express the ultimate because it transcends the capacity of any finite reality to express it directly'. In *Holding Fast to God*, Keith Ward said that religious language is rooted in people's awareness of the human dimensions of their experience: 'We start talking about God when we start adopting a basic reactive attitude to all our experience ... 'God' is that mysterious depth which is mediated in certain symbols and events in our lives.'

Criticisms of symbolism

The main problem with the use of symbols in religious language is that they are open to different interpretations. As a result, they can become:

- trivialised and the original meaning lost, for example the need to keep the Sabbath day holy is lost on a society in which many businesses now treat Sunday as another working day

Taking it further...

The principle of **remotion and excellence** states that, if we take away human concepts from a word, what is left is God without limit. For example, if we say, 'I love you because you love me', then we take away the human part, 'because you love me', what we are left with is simply 'I love you'. In the same way, God loves his people without limit or condition.

Taking it further...

The most common kinds of symbolic language found in religion are myths, metaphors and similes. As Rowan Williams observed in *A Dictionary of Biblical Interpretation* (SCM Press, 2003), 'Like all other serious human discourse, religious language requires a symbolic foundation'.

Taking it further...

By way of example, D. Z. Phillips in *Death and Immortality* (Macmillan, 1971), claimed that terms such as 'eternal life' should not be understood as literally living forever, but as expressing a quality of life available in the present.

- the focus of worship, for example relics of the saints

- outdated, like myths. For example, referring to God always as 'Father' is felt by some to be too patriarchal for the modern age; they suggest that descriptions such as 'mother' or 'friend' are more appropriate. Paul Tillich observed: 'It is necessary to rediscover the questions to which the Christian symbols are the answers, in a way which is understandable to our time' (*Systematic Theology*, Nisbet, 1951).

5 Myth

Myth is the most complex type of symbolic language because it uses symbols, metaphors *and* imagery. A myth is a story or narrative that expresses a truth when it is not known for certain what actually happened. Myths use symbolism and imagery to explain the unexplainable and to give insights into human existence. Some parts of the Bible, such as the story of creation and Noah's Ark, are regarded by many scholars as myths – attempts by the biblical writers to explain what they did not know for certain. Millar Burrows, in *An Outline of Biblical Theology* (Westminster, 1946), noted: 'Myth is a symbolic, approximate expression of truth which the human mind cannot perceive sharply and completely, but can only glimpse vaguely, and therefore cannot adequately or accurately express'.

In religious language terms, the purpose of myths is to convey concepts which go beyond simple ideas of true or false, and to try and express that which is 'other worldly' – the difficult cosmological questions that cannot be explained in straightforward factual, or cognitive, terms. Religious language makes use of mythological terms to describe apocalyptic or eschatological events, such as the second coming of Jesus: 'For the Lord himself will descend from heaven with a cry of command, with the archangels' call and with the sound of the trumpet of God ... and me, both alive and dead, will rise to meet the Lord in the air' (1 Thessalonians 4:16).

Criticisms of myth

Critics of the use of myth claim that it is an outdated concept dealing with ancient and anachronistic concepts.

In the 19th century, D. F. Strauss suggested that the way to deal with this was to shift the focus of myth from the story of a *miraculous occurrence* to the *story* of a miraculous occurrence. In the first case, it is assumed that an objectively true narrative about a miracle is being expressed; in the second, that an embodied religious truth is being conveyed in a story form which is not necessarily objectively true.

Rudolph Bultmann argued that, in order to find out the truth of God, religious language should be **demythologised** – the mythological language stripped away and the myths contained in scriptures removed. He believed that it was impossible for humanity in modern times to believe such outdated stories: 'It is impossible to use electric light and the wireless and to avail ourselves of modern medical and surgical discoveries and, at the same time, to believe in the New Testament world of demons and spirits.'

The symbolic elements of bread and wine

Taking it further...

Several biblical stories are regarded by some scholars as myths (often controversially), including the Tower of Babel, Job, Jonah, the virgin birth, and the resurrection of Jesus. Most liberal Christians do not believe it to be necessary to hold to the factual truth of these narratives, although fundamentalists maintain all are literally true. Some Christians feel able to reject, say, the literal truth of the virgin birth, whilst maintaining that the resurrection of Jesus is essential to the meaning of the gospel.

In a similar but perhaps less elegant vein, Richard Dawkins commented in *The God Delusion* (Bantam, 2006): '... much of the Bible is ... just plain weird, as you would expect of a chaotically cobbled-together anthology of disjointed documents, composed, revised, translated, distorted and 'improved' by hundreds of anonymous authors ...'.

Significantly, the difference between Bultmann and Dawkins is that Bultmann still maintained that there was truth to be extracted from the mythological narrative once the myth was stripped away. He argued that it was necessary to access the *kerygma*, or the abiding truth of the revelatory, authoritative word, which was the real tool in kindling faith, and to do this religious language must be demythologised. However, for many, all Bultmann did was to secularise the New Testament.

Others have argued in support of myth, claiming that, since religious language is anti-realist, it is not concerned with making true or false statements about objective reality. J. W. Rogerson in *A Dictionary of Biblical Interpretation* (SCM Press, 1990) wrote: 'Because myths have their birth not in logic but in intuitions of transcendence, they are of value to traditions that seek to describe the action of the other worldly in the present world'.

Myths can also be seen as being part of a religious language game and it is important to understand how they should be interpreted rather than being concerned to establish what the facts of the matter concerned actually are.

Language game theory: a postmodern view

There has been movement away from the notion that language is just concerned to describe or 'picture' things. In *Philosophical Investigations* (Blackwell, 1953), Ludwig Wittgenstein advocated a functional theory of meaning, namely that words and language are part of an 'anti-realist' or postmodern approach to language. He argued that language statements (including religious ones), are not intended to be true or false for everyone, but only for those who are within that form of life. For example, a scientific statement would be true or false for a scientist but not, necessarily, for an artist.

All language is, therefore, a game. In every 'form of life', by which he meant, for instance, science, mathematics, poetry, sport and religion, words and phrases are used within the context of the subject area – the 'game'. All forms of life have their own language and have their own rules concerning meaning. The language in the game is non-cognitive – it is not about making universally true statements, but about communicating meaning to other players in the same game.

Language can be correctly or incorrectly used within the rules of the game, but its primary purpose is not to make factual statements. The player of one language game cannot criticise the player of another, or enter into a game without first learning the rules and conventions of the language of that form of life, since each game has its own 'criteria of coherence', which can only be understood by playing the right game by the right rules.

Taking it further...

Peter Vardy, in *The Puzzle of God* (Fount, 1995), observed: 'The truth of an anti-realist claim is based on coherence. 'God exists' is true not because the word 'God' refers to an everlasting being or a timeless substance, but rather because the phrase 'God exists' has a use and a purpose within the form of life of the believing community.'

Taking it further...

Wittgenstein was not concerned with the truth or falsity of a statement, but with the way it is used and the function it performs. He wrote: 'Don't ask for the meaning, ask for the use'.

For example, words like 'in' or 'out' in cricket have a totally different meaning from the same words used in poetry. They are being used in different language games. The issue arises very powerfully when dealing with religious language. Wittgenstein observed:

> Suppose someone was a believer and said: 'I believe in a Last Judgement,' and I said, 'Well, I'm not so sure. Possibly', you would say that there was an enormous gulf between us. If he said, 'There is a German aeroplane overhead, and I said, 'Possibly, I'm not so sure,' you'd say we were fairly near... Suppose someone is ill and he says: 'This is a punishment', and I say: 'If I'm ill, I don't think of punishment at all.' If you say, 'Don't you believe the opposite?' – you can call it believing the opposite, but it is entirely different from what we would normally call believing the opposite. I think differently, in a different way. I say different things to myself. I have a different picture.

Ludwig Wittgenstein

As far as religious language is concerned, Wittgenstein was suggesting that it is meaningful when understood within the context of its own language game. Those who don't play the game will hear religious language and misunderstand it. He called this a 'category mistake'. For example, if a believer speaks of their 'soul' and a scientist then tries to find it as a physical object, this would be a clash of language games and this would be '... a blunder that's too big...' In the examples above, the response 'Possibly' in response to the question of whether there is a German aeroplane overhead is quite appropriate: it may or may not be a German aeroplane, and whether it is or not is at some stage empirically verifiable. However, to be in doubt over the possibility of a Last Judgement is another matter – it is of infinite significance and is not a question of simply verifying empirical evidence. To think of illness in relation to punishment is to engage in a particular type of thinking which has an effect on how a person lives. It is whether a person even considers that they *might* be related. Peter Vardy in *The Puzzle of God* (Fount, 1995), observed: '...in this way of thinking, God exists. God really, really, truly, truly exists. But God does not exist as a creator who is distinct from the world; he is not some being who is apart from the world and who sustains and acts in it. God is instead a reality within the believing community.'

Taking it further...

Perhaps the most famous example of a language game would be the creation/evolution debate. The biblical account of creation seems at odds with the scientific notion of evolution. However, they come from different games and one cannot prove or disprove the other.

Advantages of the language game theory

- It highlights the non-cognitive nature of religious language.

- It distinguishes it from other types of language.

- Language games provide boundaries for the correct use of language.

- Believers can be initiated into the rules of language.

- Language games defend language against criticisms from other 'forms of life', since truth is understood as relative and statements are to be judged against their context and not on whether they are inherently or objectively true or false.

Weaknesses of the language game theory

- Language games do not allow for believers' claims to be empirically tested.

- Religious language alienates those outside the game.

- The rules of the games cannot be changed to allow outsiders in.

Conclusion

As far as religious language is concerned, there is no single theory that satisfies everyone. Religious language is highly complex and, though it gives us no definitive truth, nevertheless offers us revealing insights into the nature of human existence and the quest to find, and understand, God. Peter Vardy observes: 'In finding the value of religious language, the individual finds God. Believers do not discover religious truths – they make them'.

CHAPTER 3
Ethical concepts

3.1 Critiques of the relationship between religion and morality

Key Ideas

- The nature of the connection between religion and morality

- The Euthyphro dilemma and key episodes in biblical morality

- The demands of religious morality

- Richard Dawkins and the 'virus of religion'

The association between religion and morality is a complex one, although it is nevertheless one which is, to a considerable extent, taken for granted – if religious teaching were stripped of its moral content, in many cases we would be left with very thin sacred texts and preachers would have rather less to teach on from the pulpit. However, there are many aspects to the association which philosophers and theologians have identified as problematic, including:

- Is it possible to be religious but not moral?
- Is it possible to be moral but not religious?
- What is the relationship between God and goodness?
- Does the existence of a moral law presuppose the existence of a supreme moral lawgiver?
- If God does not exist, then is everything permissible?
- How far does the moral teaching of religions accurately reflect what may be thought to be the moral will and intentions of God?

These issues are further highlighted by matters that are raised about the *nature* of religious morality. For example:

- Moral teaching based on scripture is unreliable because sacred texts are culturally relative and era dependent. The moral teaching they offer is not intended to provide eternal moral values and treating them as such leads to problems of interpretation.
- If religious believers are morally good only in the hope of receiving divine reward and avoiding punishment, is this genuine goodness?

Taking it further...

'One of the fundamental differences between a religious and a non-religious person is in their perception of morality. Many religionists maintain that morality is a gift from a supernatural deity and that, to be moral, we must obey the supposed demands of that deity who is alleged to have either written or inspired a "holy book" in which he makes his demands known. Concurrent with this is a belief in everlasting torment for those who dare to question the deity's demands. Non-believers, by contrast, recognise that morality is based on human needs. Thus, morality is designed to benefit humans rather than to serve an imaginary god.' *(The Immorality of Religious Morality* by Jon Nelson http://www.atheistalliance.org/library/nelson-immorality)

- Religious moral teachings derive from secular moral values, not the other way round. They are given religious significance to increase their authority.
- Too much pressure is put on religious believers to live up to unrealistic standards of goodness.
- The demands of religious morality are sometimes counter-intuitive.
- Society only appeals to religious morality in times of crisis, not for guidance on daily moral living.
- Resisting moral change in the name of religion can prevent moral progress.

The connection between religion and morality

The first question to consider is whether morality in some way demands the existence of God. The gist of a moral argument for the existence of God is whether the existence of morality leads to proof of the existence of God. It is therefore important to establish first whether a moral law exists, or anything that can be considered to be 'good'. The existence of an objective moral law seems nevertheless to be taken for granted by those who support the moral argument, although it is arguable that moral commands are anything but objective.

In the **Summa Theologica,** Aquinas argued that the gradation to be found in things pointed irrefutably to the existence of God:

> *Among beings there are some more and some less good, true, noble and the like. But more and less are predicated of different things according as they resemble in their different ways something which is the maximum ... so that there is something which is truest, something best, something noblest... Therefore there must also be something which is to all beings the cause of their being, goodness, and every other perfection, and this we call God.*

Aquinas's arguments were based on Plato's eternal forms, or **archetypes**, which claimed that the contingent realities of which the human mind is aware are merely pale copies of a greater, unseen reality, which is eternal. In this case, the goodness, virtue or truth found in human beings and in the contingent world is a reflection of the supreme or perfect goodness of God, to whom contingent beings owe their lesser goodness. Furthermore, God, being perfect in goodness, is also perfect in his very being, or existence, hence the Fourth Way is a form of ontological argument as well as a moral argument. God's moral perfection and authority were evidence for his existence, and all lesser forms or reflections of goodness were striving towards the ultimate good which is their cause, and participate in some way in that ultimate reality.

Interestingly, the 20th-century philosopher F. C. Copleston, in discussion with Bertrand Russell, claimed: 'I do think that all goodness reflects God in some way and proceeds from him, so that in a sense the man who loves what is truly good, loves God even if he doesn't advert to God' (cited in *The Existence of God*, ed. John Hick, Macmillan, 1968). However, Aquinas's Fourth Way does not suggest how 'good' can be defined. All we know is that God is the supreme source of it and that it is his very essence to be perfectly good. Obviously, too, it is possible to question whether good can *only* be measured

Taking it further...

Immanuel Kant maintained that morality offered the only reasonable proof for God's existence, having rejected the classical arguments from natural theology and the ontological argument. Although it is not necessary to write about the moral argument in the exam, it is an important way in to understanding why links are made between God, religion and morality. Fundamentally, for religious believers the most convincing reason for why they should be moral is that God commands them to be so, and a primary aim of religious teaching is to remind them of this and guide them in the way of moral goodness.

Taking it further...

The Fourth Way refers to *The Gradation of Things*, the fourth of Aquinas's Five Ways in the *Summa Theologica*.

by reference to the divine. Copleston maintained that it was necessary to refer to God in order to be able to distinguish between good and evil, whilst Russell argued: 'I love the things that I think are good, and I hate the things that I think are bad. I don't say that these things are good because they participate in the Divine goodness' (ibid.).

The Euthyphro dilemma and key episodes in biblical morality

The nature of the relationship between religion and morality – and indeed, whether there is one at all – is a vital question for religious believers to resolve. If at least part of what believing in God means is to live in obedience to his will and his law, then the way in which God makes moral commands is crucial to understanding how man should respond to them. R. B. Braithwaite claimed that to be religious and to make religious claims is to be committed to a set of moral values. He used the instance of religious conversion, which includes a reorientation of the will, to illustrate this point, arguing that religious language is the language of morality and that religious believers have committed themselves to particular ways of behaving. This includes refraining from some actions and fulfilling others. However, how do we know what believers are committed to?

For a religious believer, even if you get away with the most outrageous crimes on earth, you will be punished by God in the hereafter (who will also reward those who have resisted the temptation to do wrong). Therefore, even if you think that you can get away without earthly punishment, it is not in your eschatological interest to do so! On the other hand, if there is no God to support the demands of the moral law, then there is no threat of punishment or promise of reward, and so morality is meaningless. This is an existentialist view; if God does not exist, then everything is permitted.

Critiques of the link between religion and morality may take many forms: sociological, such as those offered by Marx or Durkheim; psychological, such as those of Jung or Freud; or the simple problem of how to distinguish between the moralities of different religions, are just a few such examples. In its simplest form, however, the moral critique observes that the moral demands apparently made by God – and supported by his followers – lead to absurd, pointless or dangerous outcomes. One of the most well-known methods of putting forward this problem is Plato's famous Euthyphro dilemma:

> Does God command X (where X is a moral command) because it is good, or is X good because God commands it?

Both positions highlight problems for the relationship between God and morality:

● Does God command X because it is good?

In this case, goodness exists as something separate from God, and to which God needs access in order to make a moral command. It could be illustrated as:

> Goodness ← God → Man

God is the means by which man receives moral knowledge, but that knowledge has not come directly from God's morally good nature. Rather,

Taking it further...

'Then tell me, what do you say the holy is? And what is the unholy? For consider, is the holy loved by the gods because it is holy? Or is it holy because it is loved by the gods?' (Plato, *Phaedo*, 4th Century BCE)

Taking it further...

A secular ethicist may argue that humans are more likely to be morally responsible in the absence of God. If there is no after life, then this life is what really counts and the way we behave has real implications, not for eschatological reward or punishment but because people have a limited life span and should be treated well. There is no making up for it later.

that knowledge, whilst communicated by God, comes from outside his nature – he is not wholly good, although he may conform to that standard of goodness he receives and passes to man. Clearly, in this case, God is not the guarantor of moral goodness and in some way his nature is qualified. He cannot bring goodness into being apart from that goodness he accesses from outside himself. This is surely not, therefore, the traditional God of theism.

● Is X good because God commands it?

In this case, there is no doubt that God is the direct source of moral knowledge. The chain of command works this way:

> God → Good → Man

In this model, God's commands establish what is good, and nothing can be good unless God commands it. The answer to the question 'What is good?' has to be 'What God commands'. However, if that is the case, then the answer to the question 'Why is God good?' has to be 'Because he obeys his own commands', which seems a rather limited understanding of God's goodness, since saying 'God is good' is essentially the same as saying 'God does what he commands'. We still haven't learned an awful lot about God since he could effectively command anything he liked and it would, by virtue of his command, be good – and he would be good if he obeyed it.

The first position assumes that a moral action is one that is willed by God; he is the source of morality and man acts morally when he fulfils God's will obediently. This view effectively argues that a moral law is made right by virtue of **divine command**. The God who makes the command is an omnipotent creator of moral standards and without him there would be no moral right and wrong. This has the advantage of placing God clearly above morality – it is not an independent yardstick that exists separately of him, but is under his control.

However, there are clear problems here. Is God's commanding something sufficient grounds to say that it is moral? This has the effect of making the moral law *arbitrary*, since it depends on God's whims. If he commanded someone to kill all people with red hair, would that make it morally right to do so? According to this position it would be, but would man actually be correctly interpreting what he believed God was commanding? If we say no, because we *know* that God in his wisdom would not command such a thing, then we are saying that killing people with red hair (or indeed anyone) is wrong in itself, and so God would not make that command. In his wisdom, he knows it to be wrong – but this means that God is not all-powerful after all, because he recognises and is subject to a natural law of reason which human beings also share. God's power is therefore limited by reason and, although this may not be sufficient to lead to atheism, it does lead to a limited deity.

Other problems

Other problems emerge:

● How do we deal with situations in which God does not expressly give a command? How do we establish his will in these situations? Religious believers may argue that we do so by extrapolating from the information we do have. For example, the Bible may not say anything specific about

Taking it further...

Richard Swinburne has argued that moral values fall into two categories: the **necessary** and the **contingent**. God could create the world in many different ways, with different sets of contingent values. Certain values, however, such as the immorality of rape, murder and torture, hold in all possible worlds, so it makes no sense to say that God could have created them differently.

euthanasia, but it does provide sufficient information on the general principle of killing for us to use as moral guidance.

- Does it mean that anything that God commands becomes a moral law? Many of God's commands appear not to be in themselves moral. For example, the Book of the Covenant in Exodus 23ff includes many commands concerning religious ceremonial and food laws which arguably have no moral status, for example 'Do not boil a kid in its mother's milk'. Similarly, does God forbidding what's wrong *make* it wrong? If this is the case, then God could forbid anything and it would be morally wrong – putting your left shoe on before your right shoe, perhaps. This would be plain silly, and would utterly trivialise God's lawmaking authority.

- There are many people who don't believe in God and still make judgements concerning right and wrong which they believe to be reliable. A non-believer must surely, therefore, be able to be moral, at least in the socially accepted sense, without consciously deriving moral standards from God.

- If moral behaviour is motivated by fear of God's punishment, this seems to be a rather questionable basis for morality. If it links with God at all, surely it is better if his people obey him out of love rather than fear. This view also demands that there is an after life in which rewards and punishments are given out, and this in itself is impossible to verify.

Taking it further...

If something is good because God commands it, then what is the nature of God's goodness? Is he good because he obeys his own laws or because he is the creator of them and hence possesses a greater degree of goodness applicable only to him? Surely we should be able to judge God's goodness against some independent standard if we believe that his moral commands bind humanity to obedience to him?

The second position – that God commands that which is good – also assumes a link between morality and God. However, it suggests that moral values are not established by God's will but that he operates according to moral laws already in place in the universe. The problem of this view is that it means God is limited by laws of morality to which he responds, rather than sets, and also that we must wait for God to reveal what is moral by commanding it. He is the channel through which moral values are passed down to man.

The range of problems identified here may lead to the conclusion that morality is actually o*pposed* to religion. If belief in God requires man to accept and fulfil his will obediently, then man's freedom is fundamentally violated, whatever the relationship between God and morality. If man is not free to make his own moral choices, then he cannot be truly moral, since a genuinely moral action cannot be coerced. Furthermore, a God who demands that man surrender his freedom in this way cannot be worthy of worship. Others may argue that, since many atrocities have been carried out in the name of religion, it is not possible to claim that morality either supports or is included in religion.

Ultimately, we need to ask whether the fact that something is perceived to be 'God's will' is sufficient grounds for obeying a command, or refraining from a prohibition. Jean Porter exposes this problem in *Moral Action and Christian Ethics* (Cambridge University Press, 1995):

> If the only good argument against suicide consists in the claim that it usurps the authority of God, it follows that someone who is terminally ill and subject to extreme and untreatable suffering must be told to continue to endure her suffering for an indefinite future, **only** because it would usurp the authority of God for her to end her life. Suffering is part of life and we should be prepared to endure what we must... Yet there is something deeply disturbing about the argument that people ought to

*be prepared to accept suffering ... which could be alleviated ... for **no other reason** than that God has not given us the authority to act in the appropriate ways. Is the God of love so easily offended or is God's authority so precarious?*

Abraham and Isaac

Perhaps the most challenging aspect of either of the two positions is: If X (a moral command) is good because God commands it, does it mean that *anything* God commanded would be good, by definition? How does this famous episode fare in the 'X is good because God commands it' stakes?

> *After these things, God tested Abraham. He said to him, 'Abraham!' And he said, 'Here I am'. He said, 'Take your son, your only son, Isaac, whom you love, and go to the land of Moriah, and offer him as a burnt offering on one of the mountains that I shall show you* (Genesis 22:1-2).

If you are not familiar with this story, it is important to know that Abraham and his wife Sarah had waited a long time to have Isaac. God had promised them a child in their old age, against all the odds, who would carry the promises of many future generations. And yet God asks Abraham to sacrifice him! Even if it does not raise formidable moral questions, it is at least counter-intuitive. But Abraham does not falter. He takes Isaac as commanded and it is not until Abraham raises the knife to kill his son that God intervenes. Abraham's willingness to kill Isaac is enough for God to know that the patriarch would not 'withhold his only son' from him. A ram is conveniently found in a thicket and offered in Isaac's place.

The Danish philosopher Søren Kierkegaard struggled with this story in his book *Fear and Trembling*. Was it ever reasonable for man to be asked to abandon what he understands to be intrinsically good in order to fulfil the demands of faith? Kierkegaard reached the conclusion that it was, since faith is the highest virtue, exemplified in Abraham's willingness to sacrifice his son for what must have seemed at best a capricious God and, at worst, a malevolent one. Kierkegaard argued that we should not confuse ethics or morality with doing the will of God, since Abraham was being called to a level of obedience that went beyond human understanding of morality. In this case, being bound to the moral law of society would have been a hindrance to his fulfilling God's will. Nevertheless, John Habgood exposes the 'nagging doubt' that remains: 'If morality is supposed to be universal, can it really be discounted, even under such extreme pressure from God?' (*Varieties of Unbelief*, Darton, Longman and Todd, 2000).

Interestingly, the biblical writers offer no further comment on this episode, although many others have done so. The feminist theologian Daphne Hampson proposed a reading of the narrative from the perspective of Sarah, who immediately recognises that God does not intend that Abraham should blindly obey his command to kill Isaac, but instead is offering him a stimulus for moral debate: 'What kind of God do you think you're dealing with? What kind of God would want you to kill your own son to prove how religious you are? Don't be so stupid! She's trying to teach you something: that you must challenge even the highest authority on questions of right and wrong' (cited in Habgood, 2000). Abraham won't listen, however, and Sarah is obliged to advise God to send an angel to intervene in order to prevent a tragic outcome!

The Sacrifice of Isaac, *by Jacopo Chimenti*

Taking it further...

The relationship between religion, God and morality takes us very close to questions which are raised by the problem of evil, a classical puzzle in the philosophy of religion. If religious believers are to confront the problem of evil, they need to resolve the question of whether an omnibenevolent God is logically compelled to refrain from any action which humans perceive as immoral because of the suffering it causes, even if there may be good reasons for it, or if good consequences result.

In *God Jokes* (Slim Volumes, 2001), Philip Tyler speaks of Abraham interpreting the horror of God's command as a joke – what else could it be?

> *God moves in very mysterious ways; strange almost ... God jokes, it's well known ... strange jokes sometimes, but he always knows the joke best and laughs the longest ... In the fullness of time Isaac was born ... I blessed God for my good fortune. But then came the day. Oh! Then came the day my God commanded that I should sacrifice my beloved son upon a pyre. How could I refuse? All that I had and all that I had known flowed from God. My son was the gift of God. His to bestow and his to take away ...*
>
> *Isaac never mentions it. Perhaps his new young bride eases any bad memories.*
>
> *I am old. I doubt I shall see my grandchildren. But my God has promised that grandchildren there will be. He jokes sometimes. But he always keeps his word.*

Other biblical moral dilemmas

Interestingly, there is another, less frequently cited story in the Old Testament which has a similarly horrific ring to it. In Judges 11:30, Jephthah the Gileadite vows to God that if he gives him victory that day over the Ammonites, he will sacrifice 'whoever comes out of the doors of my house to meet me when I return victorious … to be offered up by me as a burnt offering'. Unfortunately, it is Jephthah's daughter who greets him on his return. Astonishingly for the modern reader, she fully accepts that her father must fulfil his obligation to God, asking only for two months recreation with her friends before the act is carried out. John Gray (*Joshua, Judges, Ruth*, Marshall Pickering, 1986) suggests that the story is only an aetiological legend (a story which explains why some long-standing tradition has come about) to explain an annual rite of mourning in the fertility cult. Nevertheless, that such a legend could be adopted suggests an unthinking acceptance of the morality of the tale: it is not unreasonable of the God of Israel to expect Jephthah to go through with his vow even though he could never have anticipated what it would entail.

Another sufferer, apparently at the hands of God, is Job. A righteous and wealthy man, he is an easy target for Satan: 'Does Job fear God for nothing? Have you not put a fence around him and his house and all that he has …? But stretch out your hand now, and touch all that he has, and he will curse you to your face' (Job 1:10-11). Incredibly, it seems, God permits Satan to do his worst, stopping short only of killing the man. Job's sufferings are all the more anguished because ultimately he realises he has no one to plead to but the God his friends assure him he must have offended to be faced with such grief. 'For now my witness is in heaven; there is One on high ready to answer for me. My appeal will come before God, while my eyes turn anxiously to him. If only there were one to arbitrate between man and God, as between a man and his neighbour!' (Job 16:19-21).

John Habgood observes that Job's situation is resolved, as is Abraham's, by a new encounter with God. God's right to put Abraham under such severe conditions of testing, and to summarily hand his servant Job over to Satan, is justified by his subsequent graciousness: 'The fact that God answered at all, even though he said nothing new, was what made the difference'.

Taking it further...

Notice, however, that all these writers don't really offer an *explanation* for the episode that enables us really to reconcile the appalling nature of God's command with common intuitions of morality. Rather, they explain the story away with qualification: God was joking, Abraham didn't understand or he was acting in faith.

Taking it further...

'The God of the Old Testament is arguably the most unpleasant character in all fiction: jealous and proud of it; a petty, unjust, unforgiving control-freak; a vindictive, bloodthirsty ethnic cleanser; a misogynistic, homophobic, racist, infanticidal, genocidal, filicidal, pestilential, megalomaniacal, sadomasochistic, capriciously malevolent bully.' (Richard Dawkins, *The God Delusion*, Bantam, 2006)

Taking it further...

But are we really happy with any of the ways in which these cases are explained? Doesn't God still face some serious moral questioning? Is it enough for us 'not merely (morally and wrongly) to tempt but also (logically and rightly) to entitle us to say "God does not love us" or even "God does not exist"?' (Anthony Flew, *Theology and Falsification*, from the journal *University*, 1950).

The demands of religious morality

R. A. Sharpe puts forward a strong 'moral case against religious belief' in his book of that title (SCM, 1997), challenging what he claims to be a misconception that if more people believed in God there would be less immorality. 'We are predisposed to think of religion and morality as intimately connected', he writes, 'and are reluctant to condemn as immoral even moral views which are confused, inconsistent and which cause human suffering'. Sharpe makes a particular case against the Roman Catholic prohibition on contraception – 'Is it remotely conceivable that God should be interested in whether people use a condom rather than the rhythm method of contraception?' he asks.

Put this way, it does seem absurd, and there are many other, perhaps more serious issues, which could lead to similar questions. Traditional interpretations of Islamic law (*Shariah*) prescribe severe punishments for *zina*, or extramarital sex, by both men and women, punishable by up to 100 lashes, while adultery is punishable by stoning. Although honour killings are forbidden by Shariah law, in the UK alone 117 killings have been investigated as honour killings, leading to confusion as to whether those who carry them out believe they are acting according to the will of Allah. Other examples of religiously motivated morality which are a cause of concern to some include:

- Condemnation of certain medical services (e.g. abortion) or medical research topics (e.g. embryonic stem cells) based on the belief in the soul

- Harassment of workers and patients – even murder – at the entrances of abortion clinics

- Condemnation of certain types of sexual behaviour (e.g. homosexuality) because God disapproves of them

- Discrimination against women based on the declarations of sacred scripture

- Attempts to block contraceptive services or methods which prevent sexually-transmitted diseases, based on a religious belief in the sanctity of life extending back to conception

- Environmental negligence based on the belief that the current condition of our planet is unimportant, because the world will end soon anyway, after which it will be restored to a perfect paradise-like state

- Blaming libertarians, feminists and homosexuals for incurring the wrath of God, who subsequently allowed the 9/11 terrorist attacks to occur. (Influential American evangelist Jerry Falwell publicly expressed this view only a few days after the disaster.)

The power of the religious conscience to lead believers to perform actions which appear morally wrong to non-believers is worrying to many secular thinkers. There can be no guarantee either that the voice of conscience has come from God. Sigmund Freud understood the conscience as a moral policeman, the internalised super-ego, which controlled and socialised man but which was capable of doing great damage to his mental health, particularly when it was confused with religion. He believed that the Christian conscience frustrated the development of sound mental health, by imposing rules and taboos on the individual which had no basis in reality but in a

Members of Westboro Baptist Church believe God is killing and maiming American soldiers because America accepts homosexuality

Taking it further...

'One of the things fundamentally wrong with any moral system based on religious belief, in my opinion, is that it prevents you from developing a truly workable morality or ethic of your own, and prevents you from being able to adapt to unusual challenging moral questions.' (Richard Packham http://home.teleport.com/~packham/morality.htm)

'universal neurosis'. Sociologists propose the view that the conscience is the product of upbringing, education, socialisation and circumstances. It is therefore not inherent in human beings and does not owe its origin to God. Decisions made on the basis of conscience must therefore be understood as relative and situational, and cannot be universalised.

One of the most alarming examples of so-called religious morality, which plays straight into the hands of the atheist, is to be found on the website hosted by the Westboro Baptist Church, pithily entitled www.godhatesfags. com. 'Thank God for the Indiana Tornado ... We humbly pray for many more such visitations of God's wrath against Indiana,' one such headline declares. The abuse the website heaps on the homosexual community of the US, on George Bush, (a conservative evangelical clearly not conservative enough for the WBC), and American society as a whole for supporting homosexuality, is astonishing and it doesn't require an atheist to claim that the website, which argues that it preaches 'Gospel truth' runs radically counter, not only to secular morality, but to most religious moral teaching.

Richard Dawkins and the 'virus of religion'

Richard Dawkins, the well-known evolutionary biologist and popular atheist, has recently propounded the view that religion leads to evil, likening it to a malignant virus which infects human minds. He dismisses religious faith as: 'an indulgence of irrationality that is nourishing extremism, division and terror' (*The Root of all Evil?*, Channel Four, January 2006). Dawkins draws on a range of evidence, but he is particularly concerned with the beliefs and practices of fundamentalist Islam and evangelical Christianity, which he believes are responsible for misleading education (teaching creationism on an equal scientific footing with evolution in faith schools), prejudice and ignorance, inciting fear, and 'child abuse'. Dawkins proposes a classic critique of the relationship between religion and morality, which he furthers by asserting that it is a form of child abuse to refer to the children of Christian or Muslim parents as a 'Christian child' or a 'Muslim child'. We wouldn't, he argues, call a child 'Labour' or 'Conservative' on the basis of their parents' political beliefs, so why do we do it so easily with children? Perhaps more importantly, however, he links the events of 9/11 and 7/7 with religiously motivated terrorism, a powerful and emotive basis on which to launch a strong attack on the influence of religion in the modern world. In the programme, Dawkins quotes Stephen Weinberg: 'Without religion you have good people doing good things, and evil people doing evil things. But for good people to do evil things, it takes religion'.

In *The Root of all Evil?*, Dawkins visits a Hell House Outreach presentation in Colorado, a graphic series of scenes in which homosexuals, women who have had an abortion, a man who has had an affair, and even a drunken teenager who has been responsible for the death of his girlfriend in a car crash, are all shown as heading straight for Hell. He talks to Michael Bray, a friend of Paul Hill, the American pastor idolised by the Army of God for his murder of an abortionist, who calmly suggests that it would not be against biblical principles were the state to execute adulterers. He also visits the New Life Church in Colorado, where the recently disgraced Ted Haggard was at the time Senior Pastor. Despite Haggard's powerful position (Dawkins says that he held regular conference calls with George W. Bush) and his strong

Taking it further...

'Many of us saw religion as harmless nonsense. Beliefs might lack all supporting evidence but, we thought, if people needed a crutch for consolation, where's the harm? September 11th changed all that. Revealed faith is not harmless nonsense, it can be lethally dangerous nonsense. Dangerous because it gives people unshakeable confidence in their own righteousness. Dangerous because it gives them false courage to kill themselves, which automatically removes normal barriers to killing others. Dangerous because it teaches enmity to others labelled only by a difference of inherited tradition. And dangerous because we have all bought into a weird respect, which uniquely protects religion from normal criticism. Let's now stop being so damned respectful!' (Richard Dawkins, Has the world changed? *The Guardian*, 10th November 2001)

A scene from a Hell House Outreach presentation

Taking it further...

Kant maintained that, since all humans were obliged to pursue the *summum bonum* – the perfect state of affairs in which virtue was crowned with happiness – which ultimately only God could bring about, it was contradictory for atheists to pursue it since they didn't believe that God existed to ensure its realisation. However, they were still under an obligation to try to do so.

Taking it further...

J. A. T. Robinson and Joseph Fletcher, both Protestant ministers, were prepared to face the challenge posed to religious morality in the early 1960s. Rather than reject the influence of social changes, they found a way to make Christian morality relevant to a time of social upheaval. However, it was not without its critics, who argued that whatever society may suggest to the contrary, religious morality could not and should not change.

evangelical stance on moral issues, including homosexuality, in November 2006 Haggard admitted to his involvement in homosexual sex, and was dismissed from his post at the New Life Church and from his leadership of the National Association of Evangelicals. Revelations of this kind only serve to raise challenging questions about the relationship between religion and morality, which all too often appears to be dogged with hypocrisy.

Unsurprisingly, Dawkins maintains that morality evolves – it is not given by God, nor are we dependent on religion to teach morality. To have morality is part of what it means to be a society and to have learned how to maximise our opportunities in that society – the most important opportunity, of course, being the continuation of the species.

Another common challenge posed by opponents of religious morality is the limitation on human freedom it appears to impose. Nietzsche rejected Christianity and belief in God because it encourages a 'slave morality' by which suffering and weakness are admired, whilst believers are encouraged to show forgiveness rather than avenging wrong. Rather, Nietzsche believed that the 'autonomous man' will have 'developed his own, independent, long-range will, which dares to make promises; he has a sense of power and freedom, of absolute accomplishment' (cited in Habgood, 2000). One reason, perhaps, for this lack of moral assertiveness is that religion encourages its followers to have one eye on the next life, when all injustice will be dealt with, thereby taking away some of the impetus to set about restoring justice on earth. On the other hand, Charles Taylor observes: 'The moment one loses confidence in God or immortality, one becomes more self-reliant, more courageous, and more solicitous to aid where only human aid is possible' (cited in Sharpe, 1997).

In the light of this, perhaps the Good Samaritan of Luke 10 sets a rather more striking example than we assume. After all, the two who passed by on the other side were religious men – a priest and a levite – and were concerned to avoid being made ritually unclean by contact with the possibly dying man. The Samaritan had no such religious scruples and was able to offer 'aid where only human aid was possible'. Jesus did not hesitate to show up the weaknesses of religious morality when it failed to take into account the needs of the vulnerable and unhappy. Needless to say, however, it did not lead him to reject it altogether, but to offer what may be thought of as the prototype of Situation Ethics.

Interestingly, in those atheist soceieties which drove faith underground when it could not suppress it altogether, religious belief was quick to rise again when the atheist system proved fallible. John Habgood cites the appeal of the Soviet Prime Minister before the fall of the Berlin Wall, pleading with churches to step into the moral vaccum that would emerge as national life collapsed. 'Even atheists,' Habgood writes, 'when faced with a crisis of confidence, may see the need for something more than instinct, custom and social convention.'

Although we live in a multi-cultural world which is, in many ways, highly secular, religious morality has not gone away, and for many believers the only good reason to perform a morally good action or to refrain from a morally wrong action is because in doing so they conform to the will of God. We are now far more aware of the diversity of religious traditions and their accompanying moralities and we can see virtually at first hand how powerfully religious morality affects actions which have global significance.

However, A. C. Grayling puts forward an argument for the irrelevance of religion to contemporary morality. 'There is a widespread supposition that a religious ethic ... has to be good for individuals and society because it is inherently more likely to make them good. This view is troubling because it is false: religion is precisely the wrong resource for thinking about moral issues in the contemporary world, and indeed subverts moral debate' (*What is Good?*, Phoenix, 2003). Grayling suggests that modern society values freedom, achievement, saving money, insuring against the future and being rewarded for success, whilst Christian morality in particular values the opposite. 'It tells people to take no thought for tomorrow, to give their possessions to the poor, and to be aware that a well-off person will find heaven unwelcoming.'

3.2 Ethical theory

Key Ideas

- **Natural moral law**

- **Deontology**

- **Virtue ethics**

Natural moral law

Natural moral law remains one of the most powerful theories in ethics, despite its ancient roots. Beginning with the ancient Greek philosophers and continuing to the present day, natural law provides a way of looking at life which is intellectually appealing and in some way empirically verifiable. In spite of the enormous changes in society since its formation, the law can be applied in many areas of ethical debate. Essentially, those who accept natural law argue that all problems about defining 'good' can be resolved by discovering what is natural.

The basis of natural law is that there is an objectively ideal way to be human and that it is by this ideal that we measure our humanity. If we reached the ideal we would be completely happy, as we would have realised our maximum physical, mental and spiritual health, both as individuals and as human communities. Natural law argues that it is only by this objective ideal that we can actually understand what it means to be human.

Taking it further...

'True law is right reason in agreement with nature. It is applied universally and is unchanging and everlasting ... one eternal and unchangeable law will be valid for all nations and all times, and there will be one master and rule, that is God' (Cicero).

Thomas Aquinas

The starting point for exploring natural moral law is the thinking of Thomas Aquinas, the medieval philosopher and theologian, who, in this area as in so many others, has been very influential.

The thinking of Aristotle greatly influenced Aquinas, in particular his view that all things have a purpose to which they work. That purpose can be understood through an examination of the natural world and through the Bible, which reveals the purpose for which God created man. These things can be observed as regular events or as rules which simply govern the way things are. In this world humans are free but they are not lawless, because they live within an ordered universe and the rules for human conduct are laid down within human nature itself.

Aquinas maintained that:

- The universe was created by God so that everything has a design and a purpose.
- This could be understood through an examination of the natural world and a study of the Bible.
- Humanity was given reason and freedom to choose to follow the good, which fulfils God's purpose for them.
- He called this **natural moral law** – the rational understanding and following of God's final purpose.

Natural law is available to all, since everyone with some reasoning capacity can see that the universe works according to certain patterns and rules that do not change. In the *Summa Theologica*, Aquinas maintains that there is a natural moral law towards which human beings naturally incline, that is:

- accessible through the natural order
- universal
- unchanging
- for all time
- relevant to all circumstances
- given by God.

All human beings can perceive the natural law, but only believers in God acknowledge that it has implications for them beyond the grave.

Natural law draws its inspiration from the Bible as well as from the common reason of mankind. Paul, in Romans 1-3, argues that the moral law of God is evident from the nature of man and the world: 'Ever since the creation of the world, his invisible nature, namely, his eternal power and deity, has been clearly perceived in the things that have been made' (Romans 1:20). Paul maintains that, since natural moral law is so clearly evident in the universe, sinful man has no excuse for wrongdoing. In Matthew 19:3-9, Jesus observes that the divorce law in the Torah is a concession to man's sinful nature and not what God had originally intended in the order of creation: 'For your hardness of heart, Moses allowed you to divorce your wives, but from the beginning it was not so' (Matthew 19:8). Hence, natural moral knowledge should make it clear that divorce is wrong.

Taking it further...

Whether or not we believe in God, experience reveals that going against the natural order of things often leads to negative consequences. Treating human life without respect, for example, leads to pain and suffering irrespective of whether we believe God created human life.

Taking it further...

Whilst the laws of the land are not applicable to everyone, natural moral law is universal. For example, the owner of a plot of land cannot be prosecuted for trespassing on it, but he will face negative consequences for refusing to heed the weather when planting his field.

Taking it further...

God can modify the application of natural law or add to it. For example, the command to Abraham that he should sacrifice Isaac modifies the law against the taking of life since, as the Lord of life, God can withdraw Isaac's right to life. Another example is God permitting the Hebrews (such as Abraham) to take more than one wife, which at the time encouraged the propagation of the race.

Purposes of human life

The principle of natural law depends on establishing the primary purposes of human life. Aquinas maintained that it is to **live, reproduce, learn, worship God and order society**. All things must operate in accordance with these principles to which man is naturally inclined. For example, the first instinct of humanity is self-preservation; without this, we would not exist to fulfil the other functions. All other purposes advance a life in accordance with natural law as designed by God. For this reason, natural law proponents observe that most societies have forbidden murder, including the ancient code of Hammurabi, and the Decalogue (Ten Commandments).

Secondary precepts are rules which direct people towards actions which uphold these primary purposes and away from actions which undermine them. Natural moral law identifies two subordinate principles:

1   The dictates of reason which flow logically from the primary principle and are therefore self-evident, for example to worship God, respect your parents, not murder. These dictates must be observed by all humans under all circumstances if moral order is to be maintained.

2   Those dictates which are reached through a more complex process of reasoning. These dictates are supported by human and divine law, since reason alone cannot deduce them from nature. They contribute to public and private good but may be omitted under certain conditions. For example, monogamy is good for social order, but polygamy is not incompatible with it in some societies.

Aquinas maintained that God gave man reason to accomplish these purposes whether he believes in him or not. He also claimed that everything is created to a particular design and for a particular purpose, and that fulfilling that purpose is the 'good' towards which everything aims. However, although the natural law, instituted by God, gives man the opportunity to work towards the good in all things, Paul recognised that this was not always possible, 'since all have sinned and fallen short of the glory of God' (Romans 3:23). Men will fall short of God's best for them because this is a fallen world and man violated the perfect relationship with God and the natural order that was instituted at creation (Genesis 2 and 3). Nevertheless, rational man will desire communication with God and will act to accomplish it, despite the limitations of humanity. Any action which takes man closer to this goal is good, and any action which takes him further away is wrong.

The standard of natural law is not individual but is set against the whole of human nature and its many relationships. An action is therefore wrong if it satisfies a particular need but is incompatible with the overall rational subordination of the lower needs of the individual to the higher needs of human nature as a whole. Reason should always be the guide in balancing those desires which conflict. For example, whilst self-preservation is good, it is sometimes better to take a personal risk for the well-being of wider society. Theft is wrong because it unbalances social life; drunkenness is wrong because it is unhealthy and it deprives the individual of the use of their reason. Natural law is therefore dependent on the natural medium of reason as well as on nature itself, and is made known to humans by supernatural revelation.

Taking it further...

Natural law is immutable (unchangeable) and will not cease to exist as long as human beings exist. However, its immutability applies to the absolute principle, not to the law which expresses it. For example, although 'You shall not murder' is a leading precept in upholding the primary purpose of preserving life, the taking of human life may still be allowed to be a lawful act. Hence, the prohibition is against the *unjust* taking of life, not the taking of all life.

Taking it further...

The value of natural moral law may be that it takes morality out of the realm of speculation and preference, pointing to physical facts about the world in everyday experience.

Taking it further...

Aquinas identified three norms:
- **The discriminating norm**: human nature itself
- **The binding or obligatory norm**: the divine authority which imposes on the rational creature the obligation to live in accordance with his nature.
- **The manifesting norm**: reason, which determines the moral quality of actions tested by the discriminating norm.

Taking it further...

Aquinas identified the four **cardinal virtues** which apply to natural moral law. These are the fundamental qualities of a good moral life: prudence, justice, fortitude, temperance. He also highlighted seven **vices** (the seven deadly sins), which would lead people astray and away from the natural law they should know by reason: pride, avarice, lust, envy, gluttony, anger, sloth.

Taking it further...

Aquinas said that natural law was 'nothing else than the rational creature's participation in the eternal law'.

Aquinas maintained that every man also had a purpose specific to him that would fulfil the skills and talents given to him by God. Whilst the goal of a relationship with God is open to all, other goals are only open to some. This is potentially controversial: if some men are more naturally endowed with talents than others, does this suggest that God has been fair and equitable in his distribution of them? Do some people have no special talents? The *Parable of the Talents* in Luke 19:11-27 is overlaid with a multitude of meanings, but one may conceivably be about God-given skills and abilities and how he expects them to be used.

Four different kinds of law

Aquinas identified four kinds of law: eternal, divine, natural and human.

- The **eternal law** – God's will and wisdom, and rational ordering of the universe
- This is revealed in **divine law,** given in scripture and through the church, and guides human beings to happiness in heaven.
- It is made known in **natural law**, the source of fulfilment on earth.
- From it, **human law** or **positive law** is derived.

Human law regulates human behaviour in society and is exercised through the state and government, as an extension of natural and divine law. Paul again writes in Romans 13:1: 'Let every person be subject to the governing authorities. For there is no authority except from God, and those that exist have been instituted by God.'

Importantly, Aquinas made several assumptions, all of which may be open to challenge. These are that:

- All people seek to worship God.
- God created the universe and the moral law within it.
- Every individual has a particular purpose.
- Since moral law comes from God, all humans should obey it.
- Human nature has remained the same since creation.

Proportionalism

Associated particularly with Bernard Hoose and Richard McCormick, proportionalism responds to natural law by working within the framework of natural law but without insisting on preserving a static, inflexible and absolutist interpretation if a greater good is served by laying it aside. It allows for **ontic goods** – qualities such as dignity, integrity and justice – which are in themselves non-moral, but which it is desirable to take into account when making a moral decision.

Aquinas's teaching does allow for some degree of proportionalism. For example, he allowed that, if a man were starving, it would be acceptable to steal rather than let him die of hunger. However, a proportionalist may argue that natural law fails to recognise the holistic nature of human beings because it makes a distinction between body and soul, rather than recognising that humans are a psycho-physical unity, which combines reason and nature.

A proportionalist may also argue that the best we can aim for is a theology of compromise which recognises that, since we live in a fallen world (affected by original sin), the best that human beings can strive towards is a moral compromise, not moral perfection. Proportionalism may be seen to be more compassionate than a strict application of natural law, in so far as it allows an individual's circumstances to be taken into account. It does not permit human suffering simply in the cause of upholding natural law but also acknowledges that some non-moral evils have to be permitted to bring about a greater good. What is most important is to bring about a proportionate amount of good and evil.

Proportionalism recognises that natural law must be allowed to change and that it is almost impossible to identify laws which are eternally valid without adaptation. However, it could be said that it allows too much freedom to decide what is proportionately good and permits the rejection of authoritarian moral codes such as those laid down by the Roman Catholic Church. Furthermore, proportionalism may be thought to be utilitarianism under another guise, since it takes into account the outcome of an action, not its intrinsic worth.

The strengths and weaknesses of natural law

The key strengths are:

- Natural moral law is a simple, universal guide for judging the moral value of human actions, and the purposes which Aquinas proposes for human existence are common to all men. Moral law is made accessible by our reason, and it makes God's reason accessible to a believer because humans and God share the same rationality.

- Natural law appeals to the sense we have that morality is more than just a matter of what people's personal preferences and inclinations may be. Even though different cultures and individuals may reach different conclusions on the rightness or wrongness of a moral action, there is a prevailing sense that some things are of intrinsic value.

However, according to modern moral thinking, there are perhaps more reasons to reject natural moral law as a way of dealing with moral dilemmas.

- Natural moral law depends on accepting the view that good is what is found in nature. However, it is at least possible to ask 'Is everything found in nature good?' Are cancerous tumours good? Maybe so, if their goodness consists in fulfilling the function of a cancerous tumour, but those who experience them at first hand would be hard pushed to agree.

- Aquinas assumed that all men seek to worship God, which many would see as artificial not natural. Furthermore, he assumed that God created the universe and the moral law within it. These assumptions are not natural ones for the atheist to make.

- By giving pride of place to reproduction as one of the common, universal aims of humankind, Aquinas opens up difficult issues for homosexuals (although perhaps homosexuality is genetically explained and therefore 'natural'), and for those who are biologically incapable of having children. Furthermore, are those who for personal reasons choose not to do so, fundamentally immoral?

Taking it further...

A proponent of natural moral law may use the principle of **double effect** to resolve conflicts. For example, if a pregnant woman is suffering from cancer of the uterus, only a hysterectomy will offer a chance of saving her life, but obviously this would entail the termination of her pregnancy, an act against natural moral law. However, the primary purpose of the hysterectomy would be to save her life, not to end the life of the foetus. This would be a regrettable but unavoidable secondary effect, and so is therefore justified. However, we could never reasonably assert the principle that abortion is always right.

Taking it further...

Upholders of naturalism argue that the law ought to reflect the universal set of morals that all men can discern from the universe.

Birth control pills: against God's natural moral law?

- Aquinas thinks of every individual and every part of every individual having a particular function to fulfil. This goes against the 'portfolio' thinking of modern times by which we recognise the variety of functions that people can fulfil.

- There is no room within natural moral law for situationism, relativism, consequentialism or individualism. Most people ultimately are suspicious of a theory which is based on absolute principles of 'never' and 'always'.

- Aquinas committed the naturalistic fallacy: He maintained that moral law comes from God (a matter of fact in his thinking) and therefore we ought to obey it (a value judgement).

- Aquinas's understanding of human purpose is limited. If he claimed that it is the purpose of humanity to reproduce, how could he explain his own decision to be a celibate priest? He avoided this by saying that there is room for some individuals to fulfil a different purpose as long as humanity as a whole works towards the general purposes. Nevertheless, he still did not seem to fully allow for the fact that the fulfilling of individual and exclusive purposes may sometimes present a conflict.

Natural law, authority and justice

Aquinas argued in the natural law tradition that human beings only function properly in a community when some human beings have authority over others. There must be leaders and those who are led. For Aquinas, political authority – the right to rule a country – is given by God, who is the source of all authority. In this, Aquinas followed the teaching of the apostle Paul who, in Romans 13, claimed that Christians must obey governments as they hold power in the name of God. Unlike Paul, however, Aquinas put limits on the duty of obedience: either because of the way that authority has been obtained, or because of the use made of it. If authority has been gained immorally or is put to immoral use, a Christian is not obliged to obey.

In *Natural Law and Justice*, (Harvard University Press, 1987), Lloyd L. Weinreb argues that the social contract theories of Hobbs, Locke and Rousseau were all continuations of the natural law tradition, but with the state playing the part of God as ultimate authority. Social contract theory is the basis for modern constitutional government and democratic voting, which replaced the 'divine right of kings' whereby God handed political authority to the sovereign. The 20th-century Catholic scholar Jaques Maritain, writing in his book *Christianity and Democracy* (Geoffrey Bles, 1945), argues that democracy depends on the belief that God holds ultimate authority: '… from the very fact that authority has its source in God and not in man, no man and no particular group of men has in itself the right to rule others.'

According to Aquinas and natural law, the distribution of goods in society should depend on meeting the needs of human nature in so far as they are part of our natural functioning. Aquinas wrote: '… laws are said to be just, both from their purpose, when they made to serve the common good … and from their form, when burdens are laid on the subjects [the ordinary people in the state] according to an equality of proportion and with a view to the common good' (*Summa Theologica*). The 'common good' is a concept that arises from natural law since, if we all share the same basic human nature and purpose, then what is good for one is good for all.

Taking it further...

Aquinas made no room for evolutionary change, but suggested that man and his nature have remained the same since creation and the fall. This does not even allow room for the divine redemption of man through Christ, which has the potential to bring human nature back in line with God's creative intention.

Taking it further...

This can be contrasted with modern secular views of democracy and human rights, which are still in the natural law tradition but are independent of religion. Views of political authority which can be contrasted with the natural law tradition include anarchism, fascism and communism.

Aquinas believed that positive or human law should serve the purposes of natural law. He argued that the first principle in practical matters, which are the object of practical reason, is the last end or *telos* and the last end of human life is bliss or happiness. Therefore, the law must principally take into account the condition of happiness. So, for Aquinas, we have laws against murder and stealing because these acts stop individuals achieving their ultimate purpose in life – which is, according to natural law, to be happy.

Aquinas took a modern view of punishment by the state, seeing it in terms of a deterrent: 'The fear of penalty is worked on in order to ensure obedience, and the corresponding effect of law is to punish.' He held that 'only a minister of law can punish' as this ensures that punishment is given with proper authority, thus preventing arbitrary punishment (*Summa Theologica*).

We can see how Aquinas's views of punishment fit in with his overall view of natural law. Natural law suggests that our purpose in life is to find happiness and the threat of punishment stops us doing criminal acts which are against our basic human nature and which will bring suffering to others and ourselves. This view of punishment is **teleological**, as punishment is justified in terms of its consequences in confirming the importance of natural moral law.

For strong supporters of natural law, it is the one objective and rational view of human nature that we have and so should be the most important consideration in forming our views in the four areas of authority, justice, law and punishment. For some supporters, the way in which natural law can be tied in with a religious view of humanity is particularly appealing. For those who oppose natural law, it is an outdated attempt to work from the idea that there is such a thing as an objective 'human nature' – all there is are lots of individual human beings. For these people, utilitarianism might well be an example of a more modern and realistic way of coming to decisions in the areas we have been discussing. A middle view might suggest that, although natural law is no longer provable, and needs updating, its basis in fundamental human needs and desires means that it cannot be ignored when reaching conclusions about the issues of authority, justice, law and punishment.

Deontology

Deontological theories of ethics are broadly considered to stand in opposition to **consequentialist** approaches (such as utilitarianism), which hold that the moral value of an action – whether it is right or wrong – depends on the outcome of action or the circumstances in which it is performed. Deontological theories are based on the view that there are certain actions which are right or wrong in themselves, not in the consequences of the action. Wrong actions are wrong *per se* and actions which are right are not necessarily those which maximise the good. A consequentialist theory is concerned with maximising what has been determined as good according to predetermined criteria, for example what is in one's personal interest. Deontology, however, identifies those actions which are wrong *even if* they produce predicted or actual good consequences, and are right simply because of the kind of actions that they are.

Taking it further...

One implication of Aquinas' view on human law in relation to natural law is that it gives governments the right and duty to be paternalistic, which is to pass laws that protect people from damaging themselves, even if they are damaging no one else. An example of paternalism is the prosecution of individuals who are involved in sadomasochism, which causes suffering for sexual gratification. From the point of view of natural law, this is literally a perversion of human nature and so governments are right to stop it.

Taking it further...

Less commonly, deontology is contrasted with *aretaic* theories, which identify character as the heart of morality. **Virtue ethics** is a case is point, which identifies the necessary characteristics a virtuous person should possess. Morality consists in developing the virtues in the pursuit of *eudemonia*, the good life which derives from excelling in the virtues.

Deontology may take several forms, for example:

- **Rights**: An action is morally right if it respects the rights which all humans have. This is known as Libertarianism, a political philosophy which claims that people should be free to act as they wish, as long as their actions do not infringe the rights of others.
- **Contractualism:** An action is morally right if it is in agreement with the rules that rational moral agents would accept into a social relationship or contract.
- **Divine command ethics:** An action is morally right if, and only if, it is in agreement with the rules and duties established by God.
- **Monistic deontology**: An action is morally right if it agrees with a single deontological principle which guides all other principles.
- **Duty**: An action is morally right if it coheres with a set of agreed duties and obligations.

The deontologist is not simply obliged to perform actions which are good in themselves, they must also refrain from performing those actions which are known to be wrong. These are known as **deontological constraints**, or what we more commonly call rules or laws. Obedience to these constraints is typically inflexible. A deontologist will maintain that we are not permitted to violate a rule or constraint even if serious harm will otherwise occur. No one can be favoured and the preservation of another's life is less important than the preservation of our own virtue. Hence, for example, a deontologist cannot lie even when the lie would prevent the loss of several innocent lives. In this way, deontology is frequently associated with moral absolutism, which adopts the position that there are absolute standards against which questions of morality and moral decision-making can be judged. These moral standards are embedded in some fundamental source of morality, be it human nature, reason, the universe or a divine lawgiver, and remain unchanging irrespective of the culture or beliefs of society. Moral absolutism is frequently, although by no means exclusively, associated with religious morality, locating moral absolutes in the will of the deity.

Deontological constraints or laws are invariably formulated as negatives: 'do not' rather than 'do'. These constraints pave the way for defining what is obligatory or what constitutes our **duty**. Deontology therefore consists of two strands – identifying what is permissible and what is impermissible.

Right and wrong actions

What amounts to a right or wrong action for a deontologist? Firstly, a deontologist is not required to consider the consequences of an act; they can say in advance whether an action is right or wrong. Intuition alone may serve to identify the moral value of an action, including, Thomas Nagel suggests, limits on how to treat people, the obligations incurred by making promises and agreements, rights not to be mistreated or to suffer betrayal as well as to expect fair and equal treatment. However, this list alone does not tell us why, for a deontologist, these actions are right. In many cases, the actions defined as deontologically right are rooted in centuries of Judeo-Christian tradition. Others take as a fundamental deontological principle the requirement to treat others as rational beings. Still further, an action may be deontologically wrong if it is something we must not do, whatever the circumstances – common understanding may help identify these universal prohibitions.

Taking it further...

That which is permissible, Charles Fried argued, should be the focus of the deontologist's concerns: 'After having avoided wrong and doing one's duty, an infinity of choices is left to be made'.

However, all these methods of identifying actions which are right or wrong are in themselves flawed. Traditional Judeo-Christian morality is rejected by many as outdated and harsh, and with so much scope for interpretation that we cannot possibly know by intuition or common understanding what absolute morals are. In order for us to agree that an action is inherently right or wrong, without question, it must derive from an unquestionable source of authority – and there can never be sufficient agreement as to what constitutes such a source. Unbreakable moral laws cannot be reliably identified unless we can also identify the law giver and a reliable means of settling disputes concerning them.

Another problem with deontological morality is the focus it places on avoiding wrong-doing – the moral person is simply complying with a set of rules. This is very legalistic, although it is straightforward and simple. However, it is also limited, in that refraining from breaking a law does not mean that we are obliged to do anything other than observe its letter and if there is a loophole in the law, there is no reason not to take advantage of it. Where is the moral value in refraining from killing, for example, which is, for most people, easy enough to do?

True morality, therefore, suggests going beyond the letter of the law to exemplifying its spirit, and there is no compulsion on the deontologist to do so. Jesus criticised the Pharisees for their obedience to deontological obligations (in this case, tithing) whilst they failed to recognise what may be greater moral obligations: 'Woe to you Pharisees, because you give God a tenth of your mint, rue and all other kinds of garden herbs, but you neglect justice and the love of God. You should have practised the latter without leaving the former undone' (Luke 11:42). Letter-of-the-law deontology of this kind reduces morality to a set of requirements we should fulfil or constraints which should limit our behavior, but puts little value on human membership of a moral community – on promoting the well-being of others rather than just bearing the moral burden of avoiding causing them harm through the violation of deontological constraints.

Immanuel Kant

Of all forms of deontology, that of Immanuel Kant continues to feature prominently in any discussion of what constitutes right action. Kant's moral theory rests on the premise that the reason for performing any given action is that it is morally obligatory to do so. This is the only correct motivation for an action and indicates that simply following the correct moral rules is often not sufficient – instead, we must also have the correct motivation. In exceptional cases, this may allow a person who has broken a moral rule not to be considered to have acted immorally if they were motivated to adhere to some correct moral duty. Correct duties and obligations are, however, determined objectively and absolutely, not subjectively, otherwise they would be reduced to personal preferences, not universal obligations.

Kant espoused a deontological approach to ethics, judging morality by examining the nature of actions and the will of their agents rather than by the goals they achieved. A primary reason for adopting this approach is that we cannot control consequences because we cannot control the future, however hard we may try.

Taking it further...

Jesus taught that there was more to genuine goodness than doing the obviously good: 'If you love those who love you, what reward will you get? Are not even the tax collectors doing that? And if you greet only your brothers, what are you doing more than others? Do not even pagans do that? Be perfect, therefore, as your heavenly Father is perfect.' (Matthew 5:46-48)

Taking it further...

Whilst Kant was not unconcerned about the outcome, since he effectively argued a form of the golden rule – 'Do to others what you would have them do to you' (Matthew 7:12) – he insisted that the moral evaluation of actions could not take consequences into consideration.

Furthermore, he believed that, since all men possess reason and a conscience, it would be possible for all people to arrive at an understanding of moral truths independent of experience. Morality was *a priori*, not *a posteriori*, and, because reason was universal, moral reasoning would lead to the same results over and over again. The acceptance of other guides to morality, such as utilitarian principles, Kant called **heteronomy** – literally 'an other law' – which he claimed was always mistaken.

Kant argued that the universe is essentially just and that the moral law would be satisfied (the good rewarded and the bad punished) in a *post-mortem* existence. To this end, he claimed, the existence of God is a necessary requirement of a just universe and for the moral law to be balanced. He attempted to discover the rational principle that would stand as a **categorical imperative**, grounding all other ethical judgements. The imperative would have to be categorical rather than **hypothetical**, since true morality should not depend on individual likes and dislikes or on abilities, opportunities or other external circumstances. Kant's distinction between these two imperatives is vital. He believed that moral commands are not hypothetical imperatives that tell us how to achieve a particular end. For example, if someone asks me how to get to Putney, I would say, 'Take the train from Waterloo'. If they follow this they will achieve their end, which is to get to Putney. A categorical imperative, however, is an end in itself. It expresses our absolute and unconditional duty to act without condition in a certain way and Kant considered it to be of supreme importance.

Kant maintained that 'it is impossible to conceive of anything at all in the world, or even out of it, which can be taken as good without qualification, except a good will'. A good will could be cultivated by use of reason and by working to be rid of those tendencies which make rational decision-making impossible. Personal preferences lead to hypothetical imperatives, or commands that have a reason behind them: 'If you want to be well liked, be generous to others'. This does not espouse generosity as an *a priori* principle, but offers a reason why one should be generous. Kant argued that, whilst personal preferences and inclinations were not necessarily wrong, they could not be trusted as a reliable guide to what was morally right. Essentially, he argued that if we act according to our duty in any given circumstances, we will act rightly. Duty supersedes personal inclinations and unworthy motives.

The principle of universalisability

Kant was concerned to find *the* categorical imperative which would provide the fundamental moral groundwork for all actions and he found this in the principle of universalisability. He formulated the principle in his *Formula of the Law of Nature,* which demands that human beings 'act in such a way that their actions might become a universal law'. If the rule or maxim governing our actions cannot be universalised, then it is not morally acceptable, and if you cannot will that everyone follow the same rule, then it is not a moral rule.

Universalisable principles are those which apply not just in specific cases but to everyone. 'Don't run so fast!' applies just to the person who is running, but 'Be kind!' can be applied to everyone without logical contradiction. Similarly, 'Be fair to your customers so they will come back to your shop' is not a universalisable principle as it seeks to achieve an end – continued custom – whereas 'Be fair to your customers' is a principle which could be applied to every shopkeeper irrespective of circumstances.

Immanuel Kant (1724–1804)

Taking it further...

Kant used the example of the institution of promising to illustrate his maxim. If, having promised to repay a loan, I see something I want to buy, but to do so would mean spending the money I should be repaying, I would not be acting on the universalisable principle 'Keep your promises' but would presumably be advocating another principle – 'Keep your promises unless doing so would deprive me of something I want'. This latter principle is clearly not universalisable, or the whole institution of promising would break down.

Kant's *Formula of Kingdom Ends* laid down the principle that every action should be undertaken as if the individual were 'a law-making member of a kingdom of ends.' This should ensure that every individual appreciates how significant is the part they play in establishing moral guidelines and rules. The *Formula of the End in Itself* said that an act must ensure that human beings are valued as ends in themselves and not as the means to an end. Hence, their intrinsic value, rather than their potential instrumental value (their value as a means to achieving an end), is recognised. Kant clearly placed great faith in human beings being able to work rationally to such a conclusion and to be able to act freely according to principles. He placed great value on respect for people, who, unlike things, are never merely of instrumental value, but of intrinsic value. This allows deontology to acknowledge human rights and justice as inviolable, something which utilitarianism overlooks. Finally, the *Formula of Autonomy* demanded that a genuine moral maxim be the action of a free moral agent.

Kant identified the performance of an individual's duty precisely because it *is* his duty as the 'greatest perfection of a human being'. At the heart of Kant's deontology is the distinction between those actions which are performed to achieve a desired end and those morally obligatory actions which apply to all rational beings irrespective of their desires. For Kant, actions of this latter kind are morally superior to all others: 'The distinction between a good man and one who is evil … must depend upon … which of the two incentives he makes the condition of the other.' The evil man, Kant maintained, does his duty only as long as it corresponds with what he feels is in his own best interests, whilst the good person when faced with a conflict between self-interest and obligation, chooses to do his duty. No other reason for acting morally is necessary, and in response to the question 'Why be moral?' the answer 'Because it is moral' is quite sufficient.

Contrary to some misunderstandings of his moral theory, Kant did not suggest that divine reward was the justification for acting morally: 'Morality must not lower herself. Her own nature must be her recommendation. All else, even divine reward, is as nothing beside her… Moral grounds of impulse ought to be presented by themselves and for themselves'. There could, therefore, be no grounds on which morality and self-interest could coincide. Rewards and punishments may offer additional reasons for doing what we ought to do, but they cannot constitute the only reason for doing so. In this way, Kant defines virtue as being the good will which inclines towards the fulfilment of duty.

Prima facie duties

Duty-based morality enjoyed some revival in the 20th century in the form of *prima facie* duties. W. D. Ross argued that the notion of acting out of motivation is incoherent as we cannot choose *why* we act, we can only choose *how* we will act. Nevertheless, Ross did not believe that the consequences of an action are the only way to judge the morality of that action. Other things matter too – so many things that it is impossible to definitively enumerate them. However, among the things which matter are beneficence (helping others), self-improvement (developing our talents), and treating people justly.

What we actually do will be affected by various things which have previously occurred: we may owe a debt of gratitude to someone, we may have made a

Taking it further...

It is important not to assume that Kant's deontological system means the abandonment of free will and the ability to perform a genuinely free moral action. It is still the choice of an agent whether or not to perform their duty. They may recognise it as morally good but still choose not to act in accordance with it.

Taking it further...

Unlike Aristotle, Kant assumes that moral duties already exist and that a virtuous character is tested and refined by their willingness to fulfil those duties rather than being trained to act and feel in particular ways.

W. D. Ross, in 1929

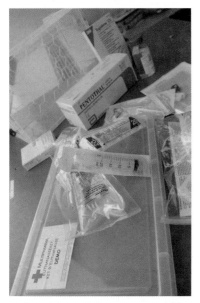

Euthanasia kits available to doctors in Belgium – should individuals have the right to choose whether they live or die?

promise to one individual, or we may have a privileged and responsible relationship with another. Ross calls these *prima facie* duties – duties to repay acts of generosity or to help those who are dependent upon us. However, we cannot tell in advance what the relevant *prima facie* duty will be, only the situation we are in will reveal it and some element of judgement will be necessary before we can decide. *Prima facie* duties are not ranked in order of importance but are an amorphous list of things which, in some way, make a difference. A conflict between two *prima facie* duties does not negate one or both of them but is rather a conflict between two things which *do* matter, and which is resolved, not by discarding one or other, but by making a decision about which matters more in the particular situation. The only way we can come to any moral knowledge, according to Ross, is through moral experience, since we only learn from experience when certain moral duties matter and when they are less important.

Although Ross may be thought to offer something of a middle way between consequentialism and absolutist deontology, his approach may be criticised for its lack of attention to the issue of rights. If we cannot tell in advance which duties are most important, than all duties are open to subjective evaluation and it is impossible to claim that in some cases rights decide the issue – the right to life, for example, or the right to a fair trial. However, the notion of *prima facie* duties injects some flexibility into Kant's theory. Duties which may have been valid in the 18th century are not necessarily valid today, whilst others have taken their place. The duties which apply to a soldier on the battlefield are different from those which face a teacher in the classroom and a surgeon in the operating theatre, as are the obligations entailed by a parent and their child. It is only if we reject the notion of duties altogether, believing them to be incoherent in an age of individualism, that deontology of any sort will fail.

Many utilitarian philosophers offered critiques of deontology. Jeremy Bentham criticised deontology on the grounds that it is essentially an intellectualised version of popular morality, and that the unchanging principles that deontologists attribute to natural law or universal reason are really a matter of subjective opinion. In the 19th century, John Stuart Mill argued that deontologists generally fail to specify which principles should take precedence when rights and duties conflict, so that deontology cannot offer complete moral guidance.

Shelly Kagan supports Mill and Bentham, arguing that, whilst under deontology individuals are bound by **constraints** (such as the requirement not to kill), they are also given **options** (such as the right not to give money to charity). Deontology can therefore lead to a decrease in moral goodness, even though it appears to be based around imposing constraints on moral behaviour. Utilitarianism, on the other hand, always requires that the individual maximise the good.

Strengths of the theory

- Motivation is valued over consequences, which are beyond our control. An immoral motive cannot be justified by unforeseen good consequences, but a good motive is, in itself, worthy of value.

- It is a humanitarian principle in which all men are considered to be of equal value and worthy of protection.

- Justice is always an absolute, even if the majority of people do not benefit.

- It recognises the value of moral absolutes that do not change with time or culture. There must surely be some things which are beyond fad or fashion.

- It provides objective guidelines for making moral decisions, without the need for lengthy calculation of possible outcomes.

Weaknesses of the theory

- Moral obligations appear arbitrary or inexplicable except by reference to duty. In reality, our decision-making is influenced by many more factors, and it is indeed questionable whether duty is as good a motive as Kant suggested.

- How far can a good will or motive mitigate a disastrous outcome? Furthermore, are we really only concerned to know the *form* of moral behaviour (duty, for example) or do we want to know more about its *content*? Are we satisfied with being told 'Do your duty' without understanding why?

- When taken to its logical extreme the principle of universalisability is absurd. Not all things if universalised would be moral: for example, 'Every person wearing black shoes should tie the left lace first' or 'All girls with red hair should wear green on Thursdays' could be universalised, but that does not make them moral commands. Furthermore, it is possible to invite a maxim which can be simply universalised without contradiction, but which would involve an arguably immoral action, for example 'Do not break promises, except to men named James'. Thus, anything could technically be universalised, and so the principle is exposed to a *reductio ad absurdum*. 'All men called Joe who are unemployed should rob a bank on Tuesday' is in theory universalisable, but clearly fails Kant's test in all other ways.

- Kant argues that what is good to do is what we ought to do and that what is inherently good and intrinsically right is the way in which we ought to behave for the mutual good of all, irrespective of consequences. In this respect, critics of Kant have accused him of committing the **Naturalistic Fallacy** – of turning an 'is' into an 'ought'.

- Whilst Kant's approach avoids the problems of emotivism – that all moral behaviour is the outcome of our personal preferences – it may go too far in the other direction, since he makes no allowance for compassion or sympathy to motivate our actions. As in the case of natural moral law, people are, perhaps rightly, suspicious of a moral theory which allows for no exceptions. How people feel about morality is genuinely important and surely morality should have some connection with what actually happens as well as with what may be formally universally universalised? What actually happens – such as the willingness to recognise the importance of promise-keeping – does not happen simply because it is a commendable principle, but arises out of real experience.

- There are potentially no limits to what can reasonably be universalised. Although it may seem absurd to argue that 'Commit suicide' should be seen as a categorical imperative, to a chronically depressed person it may be perfectly reasonable.

Taking it further...

'There is more to the moral point of view than being willing to universalise one's rules. Kant and his followers fail to see this fact, although they are right in thinking such a willingness is part of it' (William K Frankena, *Ethics*, Prentice Hall, 1973).

Taking it further...

Alastair MacIntyre observed: 'It follows that in practice the test of the categorical imperative imposes restrictions only on those insufficiently equipped with ingenuity. And this is scarcely what Kant intended' (*A Short History of Ethics*, Routledge Classics, 2002).

Taking it further...

The principle that a mature moral theory should allow for exceptions is a reasonable criticism of deontology. Only when a theory is flexible enough to adapt to circumstances may it be said to be genuinely practical.

Aristotle (384–322BC)

Virtue ethics

The great Greek philosopher, Aristotle, was influenced in his thinking by his conviction that all things and all human beings have a purpose or function – a *telos*. A complete explanation of anything would include its final cause or purpose, which is, ultimately, to realise its potential and fulfil its goal. For human beings, Aristotle maintained that the ultimate goal is human flourishing and developing those characteristics best suited to the realisation of a virtuous human being. His emphasis was not on what people *do*, but on what kind of person they *are* – although *being* a kind person, for example, is essentially accomplished by practising acts of kindness until the habit of being kind is firmly established in a person's character.

The nature of humanity

Aristotle began by asking questions about the nature of humanity, allowing that in many ways humans are like animals – they need food and air – but, more importantly, they have the capacity for rational thought, for what he called contemplation – reasoning in a logical way about those things that are not purely empirical. The end or purpose of man, he claimed, is rational thought and his highest good is to be found in **intellectual virtue.**

However, despite man's intellectual pursuit, he does still have to live practically in the world, and to this end he must also pursue **moral virtues**. Amongst these, Aristotle included courage, temperance, liberality and magnificence (one's attitudes towards one's wealth), greatness of soul (attitudes to social inferiors), good temper or gentleness, being agreeable in company, wittiness and modesty. Although these are practical virtues, Aristotle maintained that they are still under the control of the intellect.

Aristotle believed that these virtues are the qualities that lead to a good life; hence, the person who aims to cultivate these qualities is maximising their potential for a happy life – a quality of happiness he described as *eudaimonia,* which involves being happy and living well. It is of intrinsic value, not a means to an end, and should be desired for its own sake, not only for the individual but also for the society of which they are a member. A person who has developed the virtues will be able to act in an integrated way, deriving satisfaction from doing the right thing *because* it is the right thing, and not for any external reasons or goals. They will not act in a particular way either because they *ought* to do so or because they *want* to do so, but simply because they have identified the *right* way to act.

For Aristotle, the right way to act is a **Golden Mean**, the perfect balance between two extremes. It is discovered by the intellect and leads to genuine practical wisdom and moral virtue. The Golden Mean between cowardice and foolhardiness, for example, is courage, a virtue which a man is not born with, but which he should cultivate in the way that he might cultivate good health or fitness. Similarly, the Golden Mean between excess and abstinence is temperance, and between stinginess and wastefulness lies liberality.

The good person should learn from virtuous role models, train and exercise this virtue, until it becomes an automatic way of living and behaving and part of his character which he can exercise without conscious effort or will. He might become, for example, a person of courage. This may involve performing courageous acts but, more importantly, his character will have acquired the virtue of courage and his actions will be motivated by courage.

Aristotle maintained that the genuinely virtuous person is virtuous all the time, even when he is asleep, because he has cultivated the habit of virtue. This seems to accord with our understanding of what it means for a person to be good, based on our observation of their regular habits of goodness. These habits enable us to say they are a good person and to anticipate what they will do to display that goodness, even if they are not currently engaged in doing so. Nevertheless, there must be a continuous attempt on the part of a person to practise virtue and this involves an awareness of the circumstances in which he acts. Aristotle called this 'prudence' – a person must not only desire to do good, they must know when and how to do it. It requires constant practice.

Virtue ethics underwent something of a revival in the later 20th century. Elizabeth Anscombe observed that ethical codes which lay stress on moral absolutes and laws are anachronistic in a society that has effectively abandoned God, and she urged a return to a morality based on human flourishing. Similarly, Richard Taylor rejected a system of morality which was based on divine commands and discouraged people from achieving their potential. Interestingly, he argued that the emphasis Christianity places on human equality does not encourage individuals to strive to be great but rather advocates a self-negating humility. Philippa Foot argued that, although the virtues cannot guarantee happiness, they can go some way to achieving it, whilst Alastair MacIntyre noted that in moral dilemmas naturalistic theories of ethics are of little value as they are time-consuming and overly complex. A virtue-based approach to ethics is more realistic and applicable to people's everyday situations.

The appeal of virtue ethics

Virtue ethics has an appeal because it can be accommodated by both religious and secular morality. Despite Richard Taylor's observations, Jesus can be held up as a model of the virtuous man, in whom weakness becomes strength and death is transformed into life. It is a simple system based on universal well-being for the individual and the community and in holding up models of virtuous people it does not set unrealistic goals. It is accessible by reference to the real world, since if I describe a person as courageous, the description immediately generates a picture of someone who lives in a particular way and whose way of life recommends itself to the observer. Its greatest strength, perhaps, is that it attempts to link theoretical and practical approaches to ethics and maintains that theories of moral behaviour have objective value as part of developing a good life.

Weaknesses of virtue ethics

- How do we decide which virtues are to be cultivated the most? Why should we prefer certain ideals to others? Virtues have relative value in different cultures so, whilst physical courage is considered highly valuable in some societies, intellectual prowess is rated more highly in others. A value judgement still has to be made as to which virtues are most desirable and it is possible that even the most self-evidently virtuous person might not be considered by everyone to be a desirable role model. Susan Wolf

Taking it further...

Arguably, Aristotle's doctrine of the Golden Mean is itself an extreme to be avoided. 'Always aim for the mean' and 'Never aim for the mean' are both extremes, which would render 'Sometimes aim for the mean' the mean.

Taking it further...

'The magnanimous man, since he deserved most, must be good in the highest degree; for the better man always deserves more, and the best man most' (*Nicomachean Ethics*).

Taking it further...

Aristotle was writing in the context of the 4th century BC Greek city state, in which inequalities between noblemen and slaves were the norm, not in the context of Bentham and Mill, for example, when equality was considered desirable in a modern, technological society. Alastair MacIntyre observes: 'The whole of human life reaches its highest point in the activity of a speculative philosopher with a reasonable income' (*After Virtue*, Duckworth, 1997).

writes: 'I don't know whether there are moral saints. But if there are, I am glad that neither I nor those about whom I care most are among them' (*Freedom within Reason*, Oxford University Press, 1994). In other words, not everyone wants to cultivate the virtues or maintains that they are intrinsically good.

- Aristotle's principle of the Golden Mean is not easy to apply to all virtues. Whilst courage does appear to be a mean between cowardice and foolhardiness, is there a mean virtue of compassion or loyalty? Is it possible to take compassion to an extreme, whereupon it becomes a vice? Even where there is a mean, how do we identify where it lies? When does courage become foolhardiness?

- Aristotle gave no guidance in situations where virtues conflict and where we need rules to guide our actions. Because the emphasis of the approach is on being rather than doing, it can also be seen as a rather selfish theory, placing greater emphasis on personal development than on the effect our actions have on others.

- The virtues valued by Aristotle are essentially masculine ones, frequently associated with the battlefield, such as bravery and honour. Conceivably, therefore, his approach can be seen as chauvinistic, giving little credit to more feminine virtues such as humility and empathy. In his defence, however, Aristotle's static society was very different to our own, in which diversity and flexibility are valued.

- Virtue ethics is ultimately attractive only to those who have the time, inclination and ability to engage in speculative moral philosophy.

CHAPTER 4
Selected problems in ethics

4.1 Ethical language

Key Ideas

- The problem of the term 'good'

- The naturalistic fallacy

- Intuitionism

- Emotivism

Defining morality

Before moralists can begin to attempt to establish what constitutes good or bad moral or ethical behavior, they need to consider whether we can define what morality *is*. The branch of moral philosophy that is concerned with this is **meta-ethics**, which examines the issue of what we mean when we say that a thing or an action is good, bad, right, wrong, moral or immoral.

Broadly speaking, there are three different kinds of moral statement, all of which are the concern of meta-ethics:

• What is the meaning of moral terms or judgements?
Here, we are concerned with what it means to define something as 'good', or what it means to say 'X is good' or 'Good is X'.

• What is the nature of moral judgements?
Here, we are concerned to establish what is going on when we say 'X is good'. Do we mean that it is functionally or morally good? Are we recommending it as an action, or commanding it? Furthermore, are moral judgements objective or subjective? Are they relative or absolute?

• How may moral judgements be supported or defended?
Here, we are concerned to establish the grounds on which ethical claims are made – whether they can be supported by factual evidence or whether they are shared by others, either universally or in special circumstances. How can we know whether and when an action is right or wrong?

Can ethical language have any meaning?

A primary consideration of meta-ethics is whether ethical language can be said to have any meaning. If we are unclear as to the meaning of basic

Taking it further...

The answer to each of these questions would be a **normative** ethical claim. Normative ethics is concerned with answering questions about what *is* good, right, wrong, moral or immoral, not with analysing the meaning and status of such claims. Hence, whilst the questions given here are meta-ethical, the answers are not.

Taking it further...

This is what we mean by saying that ethical claims may be **relative** or **absolute**. If 'Killing is wrong' were an absolute statement, there would be no moral debate about when it was applicable and when not. But since there is debate about it, it appears to be a relative statement. However, not everyone would agree that it is relative – and so the debate continues. You can read more about this in section 0.0.

Taking it further...

A normative ethical question asks 'What should we do?' whilst a meta-ethical question asks 'What is moral goodness?'

A good computer is not a moral agent

Taking it further...

Normative ethical theories attempt to offer a definition or description of good. For example, a utilitarian would offer a description of 'good' as 'that which maximises the greatest happiness for the greatest number'.

ethical terms, how can we begin to make authoritative claims about the morality of particular actions? The statement 'Killing is wrong' is complicated enough, since we are immediately faced with a vast range of situations in which not everyone would agree that killing was wrong, but if we are not even sure about what we mean by 'wrong', then ethical debate will be fraught with difficulties.

Furthermore, there is arguably a difference between an ethical issue and a moral issue. The difference is hard to define but one way of understanding it may be by thinking of a moral issue as one which is concerned with relationships, life and death: sex, marriage, homosexuality, euthanasia, murder, stealing, fraud, abortion, transplantation of organs. All these issues have implications for man in relationship with his fellow men, although some are clearly more direct than others. An ethical issue, however, may be one which deals with our perception of what is acceptable in a social sense. Most schools would consider it unethical for a teacher to invite a student to their home, however well meaning the reason, or for a footballer to accept a bribe to fix the result of a match. These issues have less to do with the universals of life and death, but are still important in terms of establishing order, decency and a structured society.

The word 'good' has many meanings and most of them are not used in a moral context. I may say that my computer is 'good' because it fulfils the task that it was purchased to fulfil and because I get enormous enjoyment from using it, but I am not ascribing moral status to it, because a computer is not a moral agent. Similarly, we use the word 'ought' in different contexts: 'Teachers ought to be kind to their students' carries quite different implications from 'You ought to take an umbrella with you'. The first statement is prescribing a particular mode of behaviour which is based on our opinion of how teachers ought to behave and so is a moral statement, whilst the second recommends a course of action on the basis of certain objective facts.

Essentially, 'good' is used in relation to a set of standards and is hence a **descriptive** word. If I describe a dress, computer, bottle of wine or a song as 'good', I have in mind a standard against which I am judging it. The standard will not necessarily have anything to do with preference, but with a standard that has been predetermined as the norm within a hierarchy ranging from the ultimate – the highest good of its type – to the lowest evaluation within its type; we may even say this would be 'bad'. Even if an individual does not like red wine, they may still be in a position to judge whether a bottle is good according to these predetermined standards of goodness. Thus, they will be using 'good' entirely descriptively, because in doing so they are not expressing any preference or recommendation, and hence are not using the term **prescriptively.**

To use the term 'good' prescriptively means that we move from a factual statement – 'That wine is good (because it conforms to the vintner's standard of goodness?') – to a value judgement – 'That wine is good because *I like it.*' The italics are deliberate: there can be a world of difference between the two ways of using the term. The wine which is good because I like it – a bottle of basic table wine, for example – will not be good by the standards applied by a wine expert, but I'm quite happy with it. Given the choice, of course, I would probably choose a bottle of vintage Bordeaux but, since I'd rather have any glass of red wine with my dinner than none, both are, to my mind at least, 'good'.

S. A. Burns (http://www3.sympatico.ca/saburns/pg0404.htm) identifies 36 meanings of the word 'good' but observes that only one is open to philosophical disagreement: 'of moral excellence; upright'. Functional definitions of good are tautologous (suitable, sound, satisfactory, reliable, operative, for example) and so are easily interchangeable without confusion. Burns goes further and identifies 24 different meanings of the word 'right'. Some are quite distinct and belong to a peculiar, non-moral, context. Again, only one is open to philosophical disagreement: 'Conforming with or conformable to morality. That which is just, morally good'. Furthermore, Burns observes that most definitions can be interpreted as an evaluation of how well the subject of judgement measures up to the standard of fulfilling its purpose. Hence, there are clear functional and moral definitions of good or right, and only the moral definitions pose problems. Functional definitions are the easiest to understand and concrete examples illustrate them, such as: 'A computer is good if it fulfils the appropriate functions of a computer'.

However, moral uses of the term are circular: a good action is excellent or right; the right thing to do is morally good. Thus, employing dictionary definitions of good or right amounts to nothing more than saying, 'What is good is what I believe is good, morally right, excellent, upright…' By this we see that to say that something is good from a moral perspective does not tell us *why* it is good, only that the speaker considers it to be good.

The naturalistic fallacy

A key problem with attempting to reach a definition of morality is commonly referred to as the naturalistic fallacy. In *Principia Ethica* (1903), G. E. Moore stated that a naturalistic fallacy is committed whenever a philosopher attempts to prove a claim about ethics through appealing to a definition of the term 'good' by using a natural property such as pleasing or desirable. Effectively, he argued that it is not acceptable to confuse 'good' with a natural or metaphysical property or to hold it to be identical with such a property. Naturalistic theories of ethics attempt to define good in terms of something which can be identified in the world or in human nature – for example, claiming that what is natural is good, or what makes us happy, fit or healthy. These are non-moral concepts since there is nothing intrinsically good about happiness, fitness or health; they are only good if we define them as such. Such definitions are therefore open to question, because not everyone will agree that they are good, at least not in every situation. However, as Burns observes, if we offer a description or definition of 'good', it leads implicitly or even explicitly to the moral prescription that we should do what is defined as 'good'.

Making an 'is' into an 'ought'

If we adopt this approach, we effectively move to turn an 'is' into an 'ought'. It is the distinction between what *is* (can be discovered by science, philosophy or reason) and what *ought to be* (a judgement which can be agreed upon by consensus). G. E. Moore argued that it is not acceptable to identify morality with any other concept, such as happiness, because any attempt to do so will not be able to accommodate the full measure of that concept and so will always be inadequate. Most importantly, if we say that something *is* the case, we are making a descriptive statement of how things

> **Taking it further…**
>
> Aristotle identified this way of thinking about good, claiming that something was good if it fulfilled its *telos*, or purpose. The moral purpose of humans is to flourish.

actually are. It describes facts about the world and items in it, for example 'Oranges are a good source of vitamin C'. A normative or prescriptive statement suggests that something *ought* to be desired or done: 'You ought to eat oranges'.

David Hume observed that there is nothing in a descriptive statement that allows us to proceed from what people actually do (a factual statement) to making a rule about what people ought to do (a value judgement). For example, it would be unfair to move from a statement of fact that women are better parents (if, say, an experiment produced that result) to saying that therefore men ought not to be single parents.

Furthermore, **Hume's Fork** – the observation that all statements are either matters of fact (derived from empirical observation) or relations of ideas (analytically true) – supports his claim that it is not possible to move from an 'is' to an 'ought', since 'ought' statements do not seem to be known in either of the two ways mentioned. It therefore appears that there can be no moral knowledge.

Making an 'ought' into an 'is'

All attempts to move from an 'ought' to an 'is' face the same problem: they attempt to describe a situation which logically dictates what an individual is then obliged to do. However, there is no reason for us not to ask *why* we should do this. If I ask why I ought to eat oranges, the reply might be that they are a good source of vitamin C, but this is not sufficient in itself. I can ask why I should care that they are a good source of vitamin C and be told that it is because they are good for my health. But even this is not enough, because I might not be concerned about looking after my health, and certainly not consider that there is any moral obligation upon me to do so. Furthermore, if I have an allergy to oranges, it certainly wouldn't be 'good' for me to eat them, whatever their health-giving properties.

In ethical terms, to say that something is good, and therefore prescribe it as a moral action we should be obliged to perform, is unconvincing to many. Why should we seek the happiness of the greatest number, do our duty, or pursue the virtues? These may be good in some circumstances, or even most, but that alone is not sufficient to make them a matter of moral obligation. Moore distinguished between natural facts which are known through the senses and moral facts which are known through intuition. Values are not facts, but evaluations of facts. Facts exist independently of human beings and how they feel, but values are dependent on humans to exist to make evaluations. Nevertheless, putative facts can be used to support value judgments; hence values are not entirely independent of facts. For example, we may say that abortion is wrong because it causes the foetus to suffer. However, we still need to prove that abortion does cause suffering.

Almost any example of moving from fact to moral value raises the same problems. Consider this example:

> D1: 'It is good to give money to charity.' (or: 'Giving money to charity is good.')
> P1: 'You ought to give money to charity.'

Taking it further...

Hume argued that the religious and national hostilities that divided European society in his time were based on unfounded beliefs that could not be found in nature, but were created by humans in that time and place. Hence, it was not legitimate to say that because certain things were the case ('is') that they should be the case ('ought').

What does it mean to say, 'It is good to eat fruit and vegetables'?

It seems here as if there is no logical problem involved in moving from D1 (descriptive 'is') to P1 (prescriptive 'ought'). However, on closer examination several problems do emerge:

Mother Teresa visits Ireland

- Why is giving money to charity good?
- If it is to help the deserving poor, how do we know they are deserving?
- Is giving to charity once enough, or is it only good if it is a repeated action?
- Is it the giving alone which is good, or does there have to be a guarantee that the money is going to be used wisely?
- How do we define wise use of charitable donations?
- Is it still good to give to charity if I have no money to give?
- If so, does this mean I can never be good? Is there an alternative action I can perform to ensure that I can still be described as good?
- Is giving to charity the only intrinsically good action?

The range of questions which emerge here, concerning only one possible example of attempting to define good or identify a good action, show that there can be no simple transition to an 'is' from an 'ought' in moral terms.

Taking it further...

In *A Treatise of Human Nature*, David Hume wrote: 'In every system of morality, which I have hitherto met with, I have always remark'd, that the author proceeds for some time in the ordinary ways of reasoning, and establishes the being of a God, or makes observations concerning human affairs; when all of a sudden I am surpris'd to find that, instead of the usual copulations of propositions, is, and is not, I meet with no proposition that is not connected with an ought, or an ought not. This change is imperceptible but is, however, of the last consequence. For as this ought, or ought not, expresses some new relation or affirmation, 'tis necessary that it shou'd be observ'd and explain'd; and at the same time that a reason should be given; for what seems altogether inconceivable, how this new relation can be a deduction from others, which are entirely different from it.'

Moore's position is often called the **Open Question Argument**. A statement such as 'Anything which brings happiness is good' leads to the question 'Is it good that X leads to happiness?' This is an open question because the answer is 'maybe yes, maybe no', hence it does not increase our moral knowledge about X or about happiness. Put another way, we could say 'Good is that which maximises the happiness of the greatest number', but if we then ask the question, 'Is it good to maximise the greatest happiness of the greatest number?' the same problem arises – sometimes it is, and sometimes it isn't.

However, they are still significant statements which cannot easily be answered or dismissed, because despite the problems, we are not satisfied with saying that there can be no meaningful moral assertions about what is good and about what people ought to do. John Searle argued that it is

Taking it further...

Moore's argument in *Principia Ethica* is a defense of ethical non-naturalism. 'Good' is 'one of those innumerable objects of thought which are themselves incapable of definition, because they are the ultimate terms by reference to which whatever is capable of definition must be defined'.

possible to derive an 'ought' from an 'is' in the case of promising. If I say that 'I promise to…' then I take on the obligation of fulfilling that promise, so the fact of speaking the words leads me to carry out my obligation to do so. But more than that, if we hold certain things to have moral value we feel that it is reasonable to encourage others to do so to. If we cannot do so because the definition of good is satisfactory, then how can we do so?

Intuitionism

Proponents of intuitionism argue that ethical terms cannot be defined, since the properties ascribed to them, such as 'good' or 'ought', can also be defined in non-ethical terms. G. E. Moore is famous for arguing that 'good' can be defined no more successfully than 'yellow':

> 'It may be true that all things which are good are also something else, just as it is true that all things which are yellow produce a certain kind of vibration in the light. And it is a fact, that Ethics aims at discovering what are those other properties belonging to all things which are good. But far too many philosophers have thought that when they named those other properties they were actually defining good; that these properties, in fact, were simply not "other", but absolutely and entirely the same with goodness.'

If we are asked to define yellow, or indeed any colour, we can only define it in terms of something else which possesses what we consider to be the quality or characteristics of yellow. We give examples of yellow and yellow things, but we do not define yellow itself. Even the assertion 'the colour perceived when the retina is stimulated by electromagnetic radiation with a wavelength of between 570 and 590 nanometers is yellow' does not give us the meaning of yellow, although it is a true statement.

In the same way, ethical values cannot be defined but are self-evident and can be known only directly by **intuition**. Certain things are perceived to be good, such as compassion, but this is not because man reasons it to be so with reference to natural or empirical observation. Good is not a matter of opinion, but something that we can all ascertain through reason. Moore argued that goodness resists definition because people have different moral opinions without logical contradiction, and yet there is a remarkable similarity in the way in which people reach moral conclusions and even in the conclusions they draw. An inner sense directs humans to know what is right or wrong but, as Moore claimed, 'If I am asked, "What is good?" my answer is that good is good, and that is the end of the matter'.

Moore argued that, once arguments based on the naturalistic fallacy had been dismissed, questions of intrinsic goodness could only be settled by appeal to what he called moral intuitions – self-evident propositions which recommend themselves to serious moral reflection, but which cannot be proved or disproved:

> 'In order to express the fact that ethical propositions of my first class (propositions about what is good as an end in itself) are incapable of proof or disproof, I have sometimes followed Sidgwick's usage in calling them 'Intuitions'. But I beg that it may be noticed that I am not an

---

You will not be asked specific questions about intuitionism but it is very useful to include in essays on ethical language.

Taking it further...

In addition to categorising 'good' as indefinable, Moore argued that it is a non-natural property, since two objects that are qualitatively identical cannot have different values. There cannot be two yellow shirts that are identical in every way (same shade of yellow, made at the same factory, the same brand name, the same style) and one be good and the other not good.

'Intuitionist', in the ordinary sense of the term... The Intuitionist proper is distinguished by maintaining that propositions of my second class – propositions which assert that a certain action is right or a duty – are incapable of proof or disproof by any enquiry into the results of such actions. I, on the contrary, am no less anxious to maintain that propositions of his kind are not 'Intuitions', than to maintain that propositions of my first class are Intuitions.' (G. E. Moore, *Principia Ethica*)

Strengths of intuitionism

- Intuitionism allows for objective moral values to be identified, and therefore proposes a form of moral realism. It is not a question of dismissing the possibility of any moral facts.

- Intuitionism does not propose a subjective or emotive approach to ethics but it does avoid the problems of identifying ethics with a natural property.

- Whilst we might recognise the wrongness of some actions, it is difficult to specify exactly why they are wrong. Rather, we interpret it through a moral sense, not a list of moral definitions.

- We can identify a moral sense in the same way as we might identify an aesthetic sense in art or literature.

- Intuitionism allows for moral duties and obligations, and so satisfies a moral absolutist.

- The intuitionist points to the existence of a considerable common consensus on moral issues, such as the value of human life, as evidence of a common intuition of morality.

- Intuition may be associated with the idea of conscience as a moral guide.

Problems with intuitionism

- People do intuit and reason to different conclusions and there is no obvious way to resolve their differences.

- How can we be sure that our intuitions are correct? Is it a gut feeling? Is it God's direction? How reliable is experience as a guide?

- Intuition may be considered to be a meaningless concept, since it is non-verifiable.

- Hume argued that we have a motivation for acting in certain ways, although intuitionists may respond to this with the suggestion that if we feel motivated towards a particular action it is because we have an innate desire to do it that goes beyond reason.

Emotivism

A radical solution to the question of whether ethical language claims have any descriptive or factual value came from the **emotivists**. Wittgenstein's famous study of language reached the conclusion that the significance and meaning of language is found not within its meaning but its use, making it possible for religious and ethical language, along with all types of language, each belonging to its appropriate language game, to be used without fear of

> ### Taking it further...
>
> W. D. Ross identified *prima facie* duties as a way of resolving conflicts between duties. These duties cannot be ascertained in advance, but are worked out by intuition when faced with the situation of conflict. He maintained that morality was self-evident and part of the 'fundamental nature of the universe'.

contradiction and challenge. Whilst cognitive, realist, matters of fact can be contradicted, anti-realist, non-cognitive claims cannot. As long as language is used within its right context, it is meaningful and useful. How does this help us, therefore, to understand ethical language? What function does it serve? A. J. Ayer was interested in answering this question and his approach reveals some important issues about the nature of ethical language and the reasons why we make ethical claims.

Often referred to colloquially, and somewhat dismissively, as the 'Hurrah! Boo!' theory, the emotive theory of ethics stems from the work of the **Logical Positivists**, who sought to do away with all metaphysical language, deeming it to be beyond empirical verification and thereby meaningless. At its extreme, emotivism argues that, if we make a claim such as 'Abortion is wrong', this is not to make a value judgement based on an objective point of reference, but rather simply saying 'I don't like abortion'. A. J. Ayer (in *Language, Truth and Logic,* 1936) reduced all moral talk to an expression of the speaker's feelings and maintained that to say, for example, 'Abortion (or murder) is wrong' is a statement of preference or opinion. Ethical claims were not designed to make factual claims but to invoke certain emotional responses in the hearer and so what they mean is less important than what they accomplish. They cannot be justified in any rational kind of way but they do serve in some way as an instruction, since 'Abortion is wrong' is more than an arbitrary expression of opinion, it is a recommendation to others not to abort a foetus: 'Abortion is wrong' = 'Do not have an abortion'. Nevertheless, no matter how many reasons I may give for why I think abortion is wrong (or right), it is still fundamentally an expression of my opinion.

Are moral views opinions or facts?

Verifying ethical claims

According to the strict verification principle, on the grounds that ethical claims are neither analytically true nor capable of being empirically tested, they should be rejected as meaningless. Ayer argued that there were no observations that could be made which would serve to verify a claim such as 'Stealing is wrong', but that nevertheless it was clear that ethical language does serve another function. Ayer suggested that the only useful information that can therefore be gleaned from such claims was the information it conveyed about how the speaker or the groups to which they belonged thought. In this way, they were useful providers of psychological and sociological material, but it was never the job of the philosopher to engage in the exchange of such claims. The claims show what is true for the speaker, which is not the same as it being true for everyone.

Hence, Ayer suggested that the claim 'You were wrong to steal that money' provides no more information than the claim 'You stole that money'. 'You were wrong to…' only expresses the opinion of the speaker as to the action of stealing money, it does not add to our factual knowledge. Thus, it would be no less informative to say 'Stealing money!!!' where the quantity and thickness of the exclamation marks indicates a particular tone of horror.

For example, I may prefer a green banana to a ripe one, but my preference – 'I prefer green bananas' – does not function linguistically in the same way as 'Green bananas are less ripe than yellow ones'. The latter claim is a fact – it identifies something that is objectively true about green and yellow bananas and would be the case whether I preferred green, yellow or no bananas at all. It is true for everyone. My preference is not true for everyone, however, and a statement of my preference serves a different function.

Consider what that statement of preference might accomplish. Perhaps I am writing out a shopping list for someone else and I write 'bananas'. As I write, I tell them, 'I prefer green ones'. What do I want them to do? I want them to buy green bananas, but I haven't actually *told* them to do that. I've issued an instruction to buy bananas, but have only expressed a preference for green ones. Of course, I could save possible misunderstaning by simply writing 'green bananas' on the list but if they come back from the supermarket with yellow bananas they would be quite entitled to say 'But you didn't *tell* me to get green ones'. We would think someone rather silly to pedantically buy yellow ones simply because the instruction hadn't explicitly been made to do otherwise, but the example does make the point. The instruction 'Buy bananas' serves a different function to 'I prefer green bananas'.

Bananas of any colour are not usually the subject of moral debate, but the point is a valid one for ethical language. By saying 'I prefer green bananas', I have been trying to persuade the shopper to purchase green ones rather than any other colour. Fear of disapproval and desire for approval can exert a very powerful influence on the choices we make and if I say 'I prefer green bananas' the shopper may be influenced to buy them because they want me to approve of their actions, even if their own preference is for yellow bananas.

Evaluating ethical claims

An emotivist view of ethical language evaluates the way we make ethical claims in the same way. If a troubled young student tells me she is pregnant and doesn't know whether to have an abortion or not, the way I respond to her is very important because I may have the power to influence the decision she makes. If I say 'Abortion is always wrong' she may, depending on how persuasive my claim is, how persuadable she is, and what other people may have already said to her, choose not to have an abortion. If I say 'I believe it is your right to choose to have an abortion if you think that is best for you', she may choose to terminate her pregnancy. This is infinitely important, since when we are in a position to influence people's choices in life-changing ways, we begin to see how powerful the expression of our own ethical preferences can be.

If I tell my unhappy student 'I think abortion is wrong' or 'I think you have a right to choose an abortion', I am expressing the way that I feel about

Taking it further...

'The presence of an ethical symbol in a proposition adds nothing to its factual content. Thus if I say to someone, "You acted wrongly in stealing that money", I am not stating anything more than if I had simply said, "You stole that money". In adding that this action is wrong, I am not making any further statement about it. I am simply evincing my moral disapproval of it. It is as if I had said, "You stole that money" in a peculiar tone of horror, or written it with the addition of some special exclamation marks. If now I generalise my previous statement and say, "Stealing money is wrong", I produce a sentence which has no factual meaning – that is, expresses no proposition which can be either true or false. I am merely expressing certain moral sentiments' (A. J. Ayer, *Language, Truth and Logic*, 1936).

abortion in general (or maybe just in her particular situation). In so doing, and especially because she is vulnerable and has come to me for guidance, *my* feelings can powerfully impact on *her* choices. However, my feelings are not statements of fact. Why might I think abortion is wrong? Because it violates the sanctity of life? Because it is the murder of a human person? Because it causes pain to the foetus and will lead to post-traumatic stress for the mother? Even if I believed all these to be true, are they *objectively* true? Can I provide empirical evidence for the student to help guide her choice? Arguably, not. The sanctity of life is a principle, a belief, based on a set of other beliefs with which it is coherent, but it is not a fact. The student may or may not suffer from stress after an abortion, but just because I can provide evidence of some people who have, it does not mean that she definitely will. Emotivists will say that all I have done is said to my student 'Abortion – Boo!' In other words, 'I think abortion is a bad thing'.

Ethical claims as commands

Rudolph Carnap took a similar view, although he considered ethical claims to be commands, not ejaculations, as did Ayer. If we maintain that ethical claims are commands from God then we are effectively adopting this view, whilst suggesting a rational reason for them being commands. Bertrand Russell claimed that moral judgements express a wish, and R. B. Braithwaite maintained that they serve to bind the community together. This is a non-cognitive, or anti-realist, view of language, which takes the stance that language does not make factually true claims, but serves some other function.

C. L. Stevenson argued that ethical judgements express the speaker's attitude and seek to evoke a similar attitude in their hearers, but he did allow that our attitudes are based on beliefs which provide reasonable grounds for holding them, observing that moral disagreements may arise from different fundamental attitudes, different moral beliefs about specific cases, or both. We may know that a certain course of action will bring about particular results and thus argue in its favour. Nevertheless, he does allow that even our most fundamental attitudes may not be rooted in any particular beliefs and in that case we cannot reason about them. In his 1937 essay *The Emotive Meaning of Ethical Terms*, Stevenson suggested that any ethical theory should explain three things:

- That intelligent disagreement can occur over moral questions
- That moral terms such as 'good' are magnetic in encouraging action
- That the scientific method is insufficient for verifying moral claims.

Absolutism and situation ethics

At the opposite end of the spectrum to emotivism lies **absolutism**. In 1963, J. A. T. Robinson, writing in *Honest To God*, described what he called the 'old, traditional morality' of Christianity. Certain things are always 'wrong' and 'nothing can make them right', and certain things are always 'sins', whether or not they are judged by differing human societies to be 'crimes'. Robinson identified the **divine command** way of thinking, which had dominated Christian morality since its inception: 'To this way of thinking right and wrong are derived at second hand from God... They come down direct from heaven, and are eternally valid for human conduct'.

Taking it further...

Stevenson observed that there are three main ways of offering ethical argument: **logical** – which aims to show inconsistencies in the speaker's position; **rational psychological** – which aims to show why a person is mistaken in their belief; and **non-rational psychological** or persuasive methods.

If we adopt this view of morality – essentially the view that morality is law – then ethical claims cannot simply be expressions of preference or opinion. Rather, they are statements of objective fact. 'Abortion is wrong' does not indicate my opinion, my preference that women should not have abortions, or an attempt to persuade my student, daughter or friend not to have an abortion, but makes an observation which I hold to be as true for me, you and everyone else, as the claim that a ripe banana is (usually) yellow. (Not that I'd want to risk defining yellow, of course!) Robinson drew particularly on the concept of marriage and divorce, and the traditional Christian teaching that divorce was so morally wrong as to be impossible, what he called a 'supranaturalist' view: 'Beyond the empirical relationships there are invisible realities, essences, structures, whose validity, grounded in the eternal order of things, is independent of anything that can be inferred or questioned from the phenomena' (*Honest to God*).

Robinson, and other moral thinkers of his generation, most notably Joseph Fletcher, saw a grave danger embedded in absolutism. It turned moral statements into statements of fact that were true in some kind of mystical way – beyond human question – which were true irrespective of situations and circumstances, and which brought about dire consequences if violated. It was out of these observations that **situation ethics** grew – an approach to ethical decision-making rooted in the principle of *agapé* love rather than divine command. Individuals could make moral choices which reflected their preferences and opinions as long as love was the guiding principle. So there was still a law of some kind in operation, albeit a benevolent one.

The culture of emotivism

Emotivism goes further than this. Alastair MacIntyre observes: 'Emotivism rests upon a claim that every attempt, whether past or present, to provide a rational justification for an objective morality has in fact failed' *(After Virtue)*. Emotivism rejects absolutism because absolutism is an impossible position to hold – there are no facts, empirical or metaphysical, which an ethical statement can assert. The fallacy that emotivism attempts to expose, however, is that ethical statements are treated as if they assert facts. 'Tell the truth' is overtly a command to be truthful based on a preference for truth-telling, and covertly a claim that 'It is a fact that truthfulness is morally right'. For the emotivist, all we can do is recognise the power to persuade that lies behind moral statements, but we should not be deceived into thinking they have factual value.

Alastair MacIntyre argues that emotivism has become 'embodied in our culture. Of course, in saying this I am … contending that … what was once morality has to some large degree disappeared – and that this marks a degeneration, a grave cultural loss'. D. James Kennedy, in *What if America Were A Christian Nation Again?,* similarly claims: 'One of the major characteristics in moral decline in the United States in recent decades has been the rapid growth of moral relativism. The idea is now widespread that each individual has some kind of sovereign right to create, develop and express whatever values he or she happens to prefer. Surely, this echoes what the Bible says about ancient Israel during the time of the judges: "Everyone did what was right in his own eyes" (Judges 21:25)'. This is the negative view of emotivism – itself a relativist, subjectivist view of ethics – reflecting the view that once the existence of moral absolutes is questioned then the gateway is opened for an emotivist approach to moral decision-making, in which even the belief that there are moral absolutes becomes an opinion, not a reflection of facts. Whether this is a good or bad thing still remains to be seen. It is, after all, a matter of opinion.

Strengths of emotivism

- It highlights the reason why moral disputes are impossible to resolve decisively.

- It acknowledges, and in some way values, the existence of moral diversity.

- It is true to say that moral opinions are often formed on the basis of gaining other's approval or avoiding their disapproval (in childhood, for example).

- History reveals many examples of emotivist methods of expressing moral views, even if they are not verifiable, for example Hitler's condemnation of the Jewish people, and extremist views such as those proposed by the Westboro Baptist Church (see www.godhatesfags.com).

Problems of emotivism

- Ethical statements are not usually judged according to the response of the listener but on the claims themselves. 'Abortion is wrong' makes a claim which can be discussed and evaluated. Its power does not simply lie in how others respond to it.

- If ethical claims were contingent on emotions, they would change as emotions changed. They cannot be universal claims as the emotions of different speakers would vary.

- Even when moral statements are carried by a weight of public emotion, that does not provide the reason for them to be adopted, nor does it make them right.

- Emotivism effectively prescribes complete freedom of action, on the basis that everyone's opinion is equally valid and everyone is therefore free to do what they choose irrespective of the opinion of others.

- How can we judge between two people's moral opinions? What criteria are there – if any – for judging the relative merits of a moral viewpoint?

- Emotions can unite people in a common moral bond, but can also isolate individuals and groups.

- The emotional force with which a moral view is expressed is no recommendation of its value.

- As part of the linguistic philosophy of the Logical Positivists, Ayer's approach to ethical language may be largely discredited, since it proposed a method of analysing the meaningfulness of language which it was itself unable to satisfy.

4.2 Objectivity, subjectivism and relativism

Key Ideas

- Cognitive and non-cognitive language

- Objectivity or moral absolutism

- Moral relativism and subjectivism

Cognitive and non-cognitive language

Closely associated with issues of ethical language are issues of objectivity, subjectivity and relativism in ethics. A key factor is whether ethical dilemmas are **subjective** or **objective**, that is, whether they are based on personal preference or on external facts. If a moral opinion is independent of external facts then it is essentially internal, and is to do with how we feel about an ethical issue. It is therefore subjective. As we have seen, this was the view of the **emotivists**.

An objective fact, however, is related to how things actually are in the real world. We deal with such facts constantly: the chair is red; the sun is shining. These facts would be the case irrespective of how I feel, or even whether I exist at all, and so they are true for everyone, not just me or those who share my beliefs. In the same way, if moral values are objective then they are similarly true for everyone. Whether morality deals in facts or opinions is a crucial issue for ethical debate and the key to this is whether we can place **goodness** in an objective category, since it is clearly open to so many different interpretations.

Moral realism

If morality is objective, then it is **cognitive,** or **realist**. Cognitive language deals with making propositions about things that can be known and so can be held to be true or false. Moral realism holds that there are objective moral values and that evaluative statements are factual claims, the truth or falsity of which does not depend on our beliefs, feelings or other attitudes towards the things that are subject to moral evaluation.

Related to this is **ethical descriptivism** or **naturalism**, which asserts that moral value is a real, objective property of the natural (physical) world. Hence a moral judgement is either true or false, depending on the facts of the world as it exists.

Moral realism comes in two forms:

1   **Ethical intuitionism,** or **ethical non-naturalism,** which holds that there are objective, moral properties (such as the property of 'goodness'), and that we sometimes have intuitions of these moral properties or truths.

Taking it further...

Another way of distinguishing between meta-ethical theories is between **monistic** theories (in which there is a single true, or highest, good) and **pluralistic** theories, which argue that there are many goods.

2   **Ethical naturalism**, which holds that there are objective moral properties but that these properties are reducible to entirely non-ethical properties such as happiness or desirability. Most ethical naturalists hold that we have empirical knowledge of moral truths.

If moral realism is subjective, then it is **non-cognitive,** or **anti-realist,** and deals with matters that are not simply resolved by establishing if they are true or false. This is a **non-propositional** view, which understands language as serving some other function than that of making true/false claims. For example, if I witness a boy smashing car windscreens and report it to the police, then I am reporting a fact, but if I tell them that I thought the boy was wrong to be doing so, I would be reporting my feelings about it, and this would not be a fact. Presumably the boy doing the smashing did not consider his actions to be wrong, so it is a subjective rather than objective matter, even if more people share my opinion than his.

Moral anti-realism

This view holds that there are no objective values. It comes in three forms:

1   **Ethical subjectivism**, which holds that moral statements are made true or false by the attitudes of the speaker or those observing. There are several different versions of subjectivism, including:

- **Moral subjectivism:** For something to be morally right it must be approved of by society. Different things are right for people in different societies and during different historical periods.

- **Divine command ethics:** Another subjectivist theory holds that for a thing to be right it must be commanded by or approved by God. Those who hold this view, however, often see it as objectivist, since God's commands are absolute.

- **Individualism:** This view, supported by Protagoras, is that there are as many distinct scales of good and evil as there are people in the world.

2   **Non-cognitivism,** which holds that ethical sentences are neither true nor false because they do not assert genuine propositions. Non-cognitivist views of ethics include:

- **Emotivism**, proposed by A. J. Ayer and C. L. Stevenson. This is discussed in detail in section 4.1.

- **Prescriptivism**, defended by R. M. Hare, which holds that moral statements function like imperatives, so 'Killing is wrong' means 'Don't kill!' in the same way as 'Speeding is wrong' means 'Don't speed!'. Moral utterances have no truth value but prescribe attitudes to others and express the conviction of the speaker.

- **Quasi-realism,** which argues that ethical statements appear to be factual claims and can be called true or false, even though there are no ethical facts for them to correspond to.

- **Moral scepticism**, proposed by J. L. Mackie, who claimed that there are no objective values, hence ethical claims are false.

- **Moral particularism,** which makes the claim that there are no defensible moral principles and that moral thought does not consist in the application of moral principles to cases. The morally perfect person should not therefore be conceived of as the person of principle. A weaker position holds that, though there may be some moral principles, the rationality of moral thought and judgement in no way depends on them. Rather, the perfectly moral judge would need far more than a grasp on an appropriate range of principles and the ability to apply them. Moral principles are, at best, crutches that a morally sensitive person would not require and, in themselves, they may lead people to make errors in moral reasoning.

Objectivity or moral absolutism

Objectivity in ethics is commonly associated with **absolutism,** which takes the view that ethical principles can be established *a priori*, that is, without experience. They are independent of experience because they are intrinsically right, irrespective of the outcome. The grounds of these *a priori* principles may vary; they may be derived from God's will or from the law of the land, but whatever their source they are 'good' without reference to any hypothetical consequences. This is clearly quite different to a teleological approach to ethics, which adopts a more (although not exclusively) relativist approach and is concerned with ends rather than means. From a teleological perspective, 'good' can only be defined in terms of the outcome of an action, not its inherent moral worth.

Taking an absolutist approach makes it possible to evaluate moral actions in a critical way, since if an individual or group is not conforming to the recognised absolute standard or law, they can justifiably be condemned for it. However, this depends entirely on whether societies and individuals can come to an agreement as to what constitutes absolute morality, and that it is more than just a matter of personal preference or subjective opinion. So we are back to the initial problem: how can we reach a consensus as to what is 'good' that we can be sure is not subjective opinion, however many people may support it?

Moral absolutism can also be known as **hard universalism,** which holds that there is one universal moral code and does not acknowledge even the possibility of there being more than one set of morals. It is at the opposite end of the spectrum to **moral nihilism,** which claims that there are no moral truths. Although an absolutist might claim that they are right because they are right, more frequently they will attempt to demonstrate through reasoning and evidence the legitimacy of their position, for example by the moral law evident in nature, or the inherent truth of certain claims which can be universalised.

Moral absolutism is consistent with the thinking of Plato, who believed that values existed as Forms which were **universal, absolute,** and **pre-existent.** Moral absolutists might, for example, judge slavery, war, dictatorship, the death penalty, or childhood abuse to be absolutely and inarguably immoral, regardless of the beliefs and goals of a culture that engages in these practices. Many religious moralities are absolutist, though not always without attracting controversy. For example, under some religious moral absolutist beliefs, homosexual behavior is considered fundamentally wrong, even in a committed monogamous relationship and irrespective of changing norms within society. Today, almost no religious group endorses slavery, whereas in

---

Taking it further...

If an ethical claim cannot be seen as fitting into any of these categories, then the only alternative is for ethical statements to be true objective claims, which entails moral realism.

Taking it further...

A **utilitarian** approach is teleological, as it seeks to maximise the ends and to seek the instrumental good, rather than the intrinsic good. An objectivist will seek to identify the intrinsic source of morality, irrespective of circumstances.

Taking it further...

Kant's **deontological** theory was based on the principle that a moral action is objectively only that which can be universalised. A categorical imperative identifies an action which can, without contradiction, become a universal law.

Gay Pride celebrations would have been inconceivable 50 years ago

the past many communities held it to be perfectly ethical, so it is possible that at some future date religiously-motivated opposition to homosexuality might also change, thereby undermining an absolutist approach.

> ### Taking it further...
>
> Some Christians regard Christian theology as teaching a **hierarchy** of moral absolutes, a view called **graded absolutism**. If there is a conflict between two absolutes, the duty to obey the higher one exempts the individual from the duty to obey the lower one. The order of priority is duty to God first, then duty to fellow humans, then duty to property. The 'greatest commandment' (love God and neighbour) underpins this approach. Under this system, for example, Corrie ten Boom was morally justified in lying to the Nazis about the Jews her family was hiding, because protecting lives is a higher moral value than telling the truth to murderers. (See www.**corrietenboom**.com for more information about Corrie ten Boom.)

> ### Taking it further...
>
> How should you distinguish between these two terms? Think of relativism as concerned with moral values *relative* to situation, culture or historical setting. Subjectivism is associated with how an individual or the group they belong to *feel* or *think* about morality.

> ### Taking it further...
>
> In everyday discussion, people often describe themselves as moral relativists, meaning that they are accepting of other people's values. This has little to do with the philosophical idea of relativism, since relativism does not necessarily imply tolerance, just as moral objectivism does not necessarily imply intolerance.

Moral relativism and subjectivism

The moral relativist argues that we cannot reach a consensus on objective morality because moral values – what is determined as 'good' or 'bad' – are grounded in social custom and moral judgements are therefore true or false relative to the particular moral framework of the speaker's community. **Moral diversity** is explained by the fact that moral beliefs are the product of different ways of life and are matters of opinion that vary from culture to culture (**cultural relativism**) or from person to person and in different situations (**moral relativism**).

Furthermore, our conceptions of morality should be based on how people *actually* behave (*de facto* values) rather than on an ideal standard of how people *should* behave (ideal values) because there is no one right or wrong way of behaving. Moral relativism argues that moral values are grounded in social custom. Protagoras was a relativist, claiming that 'Man is the measure of all things – of things that are, that they are, of things that are not, that they are not'. Some **existentialist relativists**, such as Jean-Paul Sartre, hold that a personal and subjective moral core lies at the heart of individual moral acts. According to this view, public morality reflects social convention, and only personal, subjective morality expresses true authenticity.

Cultural relativism

This is the principle that an individual's actions should be interpreted in the context of that individual's culture. It was particularly prevalent as a tool in anthropological study in the 20th century. As a principle, it is not intended to be used to justify the moral goodness of an action, but to help understand the context of that action. Hence, it does not justify the actions of one tribe as being appropriate to all other tribes, but rather that the appropriateness of any positive or negative custom must be evaluated with regard to how this habit fits with other group habits.

Ultimately, the implications of moral relativism include accepting that there is no point to moral debate, since opposing moral claims are true in an anti-realist sense, relative to the culture from which they emerge. However, moral relativism would allow us to establish morality simply by consulting the community – although there is no room for reform since reformers would be challenging the norms of society. What is good for the relativist is therefore what they believe is good.

Nevertheless, there are several problems:

- If you want to propose a particular moral viewpoint, all you need to do is form a community of like-minded moralists. This would not generally be considered an acceptable justification of an immoral action, since just because one group in society favours an action other groups consider to be immoral, why should they be forced to accept it regardless?

- Moral relativism considers the views of other cultures to be relevant and true for them, but not worthy of engagement in debate.

- J. L. Mackie observed that the morality of individuals tends to be shaped by their society, not the other way round. He rejected the view that there is an absolute standard of good, but rather believed that, although individuals are inclined to think that there is an objective standard of goodness, this reflects nothing more than a psychological need to find such a standard.

- Moral relativism may not be clear about whether moral rules themselves differ between cultures or groups or whether the rules are themselves entirely different.

- Moral subjectivism is sometimes considered a sub-category of moral relativism. However, moral subjectivism does not claim that each culture is right in its own way but that people are right in their own way. This is exceptionally tolerant but cannot solve moral conflicts since there is never any common denominator to which to refer and any individual moral stance is considered equally valid.

- Relativists do, however, adopt an absolute principle: 'Be tolerant of everyone's different moral codes'.

- Arguably, relativists fail to recognise the similarities that exist between the moralities of different cultures and place too much emphasis on the variations. Furthermore, societies are complex and reflect many sub-groups and cultures, so there can be no one culturally agreed morality.

4.3 Justice, law and punishment

Key Ideas

- The underlying principles of justice

- Authority and the social contract

- Justice, rights and duties

- The nature of law

- The purpose of punishment

- Capital punishment

Taking it further...

Marx claimed that true justice will only flourish in a classless society, where no one group is able to impose its will on others.

The underlying principles of justice

'Justice is fairness, equal opportunities for all to make something of their lives, and a way back from the deaths for those who fail' (*Thinking Through Philosophy,* Horner and Westacott, Cambridge University Press, 2000).

Justice is about treating people equally and fairly. It is an important aspect of social democracy, where the legal and moral system of a society is the result of a negotiation between the needs of the people as a whole and the freedom of the individual.

In *The Republic*, Plato argued that justice was the way to the happiest life. He believed that all the elements of society should work together for the health of the whole, and that justice is the expression of that health. In contrast, injustice is a sickness, resulting in suffering for all. Plato believed that both the state and the individual should be ruled by reason. He accepted that, in a natural state, everyone is concerned with his or her own self-interest and that the strong tend to impose their notions of justice on the weak. However, if there is only self-interest, then society breaks down. Plato claimed that society has to create a sense of order and justice to curb such self-interest, so that all citizens can benefit, receive appropriate satisfaction and live together in harmony. It does this through reason – people use rationality to control their selfish desires and choose to obey the laws as matter of social acceptance. For Plato, justice is achieved within the state when everyone is able to live and work in harmony with others.

Equality

Justice is concerned with equality. But equality itself is a difficult concept to define. Augustine observed that 'Equality must be something other than treating everyone in the same way, since everyone is different'. There are four main notions of equality:

- **Fundamental equality**
  All citizens are treated as equals by the government and the legal systems.

- **Social equality**
  Citizens have the right to vote and to stand for public office.

- **Equal treatment for equals**
  People of the same group are treated in the same way. It is an elitist principle that does not regard equality as a human right for all.

- **Treating people unequally in special circumstances**
  Equals are people in the same situation and the same circumstances. Someone in a different situation is an unequal, who may need special treatment. Treating people equally does not imply treating them the same.

In reality, justice is difficult to achieve because life is full of inequalities. In his *Enquiry Concerning the Principles of Morals* (Oxford University Press, 1975), David Hume suggested that one could never achieve a justice system based on what people deserve, since it is impossible to agree about what each person deserves. Nor could there be a 'justice of equality', since people are unequal in what they have. By accident of birth or genetics, some are rich, others are poor, some are attractive and others are not. People are, by nature, unequal in their abilities and some will, therefore, prosper more than others. In *What does it all mean?* (Oxford University Press, 1987), Thomas Nagel noted that, despite our concern for equality as the basis for a just society, many inequalities are deliberately imposed, for example racial and sexual discrimination. There will always be people who are wealthier, or more talented, and although social democracy may seek **equality of opportunity**, in fact, **inequality of result** is usually the outcome. These inequalities cannot be easily overcome without a radical overhaul of the political system. It would mean limiting human freedom and society would be acting to prevent its citizens from making the most of their abilities, talents and opportunities.

Justice, therefore, is difficult to achieve, because the system is unfair and limits people's freedom by helping those who are born with advantages. For instance, those who are born into rich families tend to get the finest education and receive far greater opportunities to develop their talents and skills than those who are poor. Critics, such as Marx, have argued that a greater measure of justice could be achieved if the state attempted to balance the inequalities, for example by taxing the wealthy more heavily and using the money to provide better educational facilities for the less well-off. This may be ethically justified on the grounds that, although higher taxation limits the freedom of the rich to spend their money as they choose, it does not remove that freedom completely. Redistributive taxation allows the government to interfere in what people do but within reasonable limits. It contributes to overall equality.

In *Justice that Restores* (IVP, 2000), Charles Colson argues that justice is characterised by the society it is a part of. It is the system of political and social structures that enables citizens of that state to live together in harmony and security: 'A society has a foundation for justice when it observes a rule of law grounded in objective truth.' In Colson's view, if the law loses its authority within a society, then the notion of justice also suffers

Taking it further...

In the Bible, the concept of equality appears at the Creation, where both man and woman are made in the image of God (Genesis 1:28). The Bible does not refer to the subordination of women to men until after the Fall. The woman's subordination to the man was one of the punishments incurred for rebelling against God: 'Your desire shall be for your husband and he shall rule over you' (Genesis 3:16).

Inside the House of Commons; the UK functions as a social democracy

Taking it further...

Opponents argue that the system of taxation itself is unfair on those who have worked hard for their wealth and say that a centrally-controlled economy in which everyone is paid the same is even less desirable, as it prevents people from achieving their full potential.

and can be abused by pressure groups. He argues that the law gains its moral authority not only by reflecting the moral traditions of that society, but also by encompassing an objective standard of justice applicable to all humanity. In his view, the ultimate authority was God: 'For justice is impossible without the rule of law; and the rule of law is impossible without transcendent authority'.

Colson argues that the only true justice is **restorative justice**, whilst for the utilitarian, **distributive justice** should ensure the greatest good of the greatest number. For Bentham, that 'good' is pleasure; later versions of utilitarianism have other more sophisticated versions of what the 'good' is. Utilitarians would see the empirical and measurable 'good' as a better criterion for deciding who should get what than the view of human nature put forward by natural law which cannot be proved and which if, for example, it leads to a view that human life must be preserved whatever the financial implications, could lead to great and useless suffering for others who are waiting for treatment. Supporters of distributive justice based on natural law, on the other hand, would see utilitarians risking obvious injustice – in, for example, accepting a certain amount of poverty as inevitable if the happiness of the great majority is served.

Taking it further...

In *The Republic*, Plato suggested that justice was an objective, knowable reality, on which the concept of law rests.

Authority and the social contract

'It is the strongest who rule. Whatever anyone says, it is the ability to use force that compels obedience. Look at history: when power fails, the state collapses' (*Thinking Through Philosophy*, Horner and Westacott, Cambridge University Press, 2000).

There is no justice without authority and justice has no meaning if the state cannot ensure that its laws are accepted and followed by its citizens. The state, therefore, must have sufficient power to ensure that citizens respect and obey the law. Laws are created and devised by state legislators and imposed upon the people, sometimes by sheer brute force, but more commonly (and more effectively), by the state convincing the people that, under its rule, greater freedom and peace will be available than would otherwise be the case.

The law courts punish lawbreakers

Philosophers have put forward ethical theories based on the notion of a 'social contract', which citizens enter into with the state. The relationship is consensual – the people agree to obey the state and limit their personal freedom and the state promises protection, security and to work for the common good. Authority, therefore, comes from the notion of **consent**. This is a utilitarian approach to justice, as outlined by William Frankena in *Ethics* (Prentice Hall, 1973): '... the right is to promote the general good – that our actions and our rules are to be decided upon by determining which of them produces or may be expected to produce the greatest general balance of good over evil'.

In *Leviathan*, Thomas Hobbes said that, under such a contract, the ruler should agree to protect the natural rights of the people, to act as arbiter in disputes and to make laws to establish these things. In return, the people accept the authority of the ruler. Most controversially, Hobbes argued that the ruler should be above the law and must have absolute power in order to prevent anarchy and social collapse. He famously said that, without law, life would be '… solitary, poor, nasty, brutish and short'.

In *Treatise on Civil Government*, John Locke took a slightly different view, suggesting that, under the social contract, the people surrender some of their individual rights to society, but that nobody, not even the ruler, is above the law. The institutions of the state have authority because they have the support of the majority of the people. It becomes the duty of the state to uphold individual rights and freedoms.

By way of example, the American Declaration of Independence, which entitles every citizen to life, liberty and the pursuit of happiness, is based on the work of Thomas Paine, who argued that, under the social contract, the individual should be given liberty and allowed to do anything as long as no harm is done to others.

In *On Liberty*, J. S. Mill highlighted the fact that, under the social contract, it is important to protect the rights of minority groups. He said that it would be wrong for the majority to force the minority to conform to its wishes. Instead, the majority should only interfere with a minority if that minority undertakes activities that are directly harmful to the interests of the majority. Mill called this his 'harm principle': '… the only purpose for which power can be rightfully exercised over any member of a civilised community, against his will, is to prevent harm to others'.

Justice, rights and duties

An important principle of justice is the notion of rights and duties. When people interact, make choices and take responsibility for the consequences of those choices, they are acting as 'moral agents'. This gives them certain duties and rights – things they ought to do (duties) and ought to receive (rights). MacQuarrie and Childless, in *A New Dictionary of Christian Ethics* (SCM, 1990), defined them as '… powers or privileges which are so justly claimed that they must be not be infringed or suspended'.

In a democracy, these rights and duties are inviolable and belong to each citizen. Without them, there can be no justice. Rights and duties are two sides of the same coin; thus, a person has a duty to respect the rights of others and, in turn, can expect others to respect his/her rights. For example, if I have the right to walk along the street without being attacked, then others have the duty not to attack me. In the same way, I have a duty not to attack others in return for my right not to be attacked by them.

Ethicists have suggested five bases on which the concepts of rights and duties are established:

- **Divine right**: Rights given by God, for example the right to life.
- **Natural rights**: Rights that come from human nature, for example the right to food and shelter.
- **Contract**: Society agrees to limit the rights of citizens in order to ensure an ordered society, for example the right to an education and the duty to pay taxes to provide schools.

Taking it further...

This view was supported by Rousseau. He claimed that, under a social contract imposed by what he called the 'general will', the people would give up some of their natural freedoms in order to establish 'civil liberty'. In other words, the individual gives up their freedom in order to benefit society as a whole.

Taking it further...

In recent times, many governments have attempted to curb the actions and freedoms of certain minority groups in order to protect the majority from acts of terrorism.

Taking it further...

We tend to assume that all humans have these rights, but, in reality, we still encounter enormous problems with discrimination and bigotry against those on the fringes of society or those who represent a particular social group.

- **Utilitarian**: Respecting the rights of others and having your own rights respected by other people, for example the right not to be harmed and, in return, the duty not to harm others.

- **Totalitarian**: Rights can be exercised as long as the state permits them, for example the right to drink alcohol.

Furthermore, we can distinguish between **political rights,** which are concerned with the relationship between the individual and the government, and **civil rights**, which are concerned with equal treatment for all in relation to the law, religious freedom, ownership of property, education and privacy.

The **Universal Declaration of Human Rights** (1948) recognises that human rights:

- must be accepted and acted upon
- are possessed by all human beings
- are fundamental to all human life
- must be enforced
- may serve to restrict the actions of others
- in some cases, cannot be forfeited.

The nature of law

Law consists of the rules that govern human relationships in a civilised society. Laws are made and enforced by the state to enable people to live together in freedom, safety and order. They protect the weak from the oppression of the strong. Justice is about enforcing these laws in a way that is fair and equal to all citizens. It is about rewarding the good and punishing the bad. We might say, therefore, that the law is made by the state and justice is enforced through the courts.

Is there an absolute duty to obey the law? Thomas Aquinas believed that law and justice are intrinsically linked and that if a law is not just, then the people are under no duty to obey it. For Aquinas, laws are artificial pronouncements that are devised and imposed by the state – they are not absolute commands. However, Aquinas allowed that the government does have the right to be **paternalistic** – to make laws limiting human freedom to perform certain actions that cause harm to the individual, even if they do not harm anyone else.

J. S. Mill suggested a contrasting position on paternalism in his famous essay *On Liberty*, which has had a great influence on law-making since it was written in the 19th century. He put his case thus: '… the individual is not accountable to society for his actions, in so far as these concern the interests of no person but himself' (John Stuart Mill *On Liberty* ed. Stefan Collini, Cambridge University Press, 1989 p.94). Mill argued that the only purpose of passing laws is to stop one person doing significant harm to another against that person's will. Anything else that people choose to do is up to them, and governments should not interfere.

Taking it further...

So-called **basic liberties**, such as the right to free speech, cannot be infringed except in cases that would cause serious harm to individuals. **General liberties** are those that can be forfeited in the interests of society's more general welfare, for example the right to free movement.

Taking it further...

Of course, not all human actions are regulated by law. There are many actions that people consider to be wrong which are not, necessarily, against the law – being untidy, for example.

Taking it further...

In the 1990s, the UK Government issued a law requiring people to pay a Community Charge called the Poll Tax. Many people thought that the law was unfair and there was a great deal of protesting and rioting. Eventually, the Government withdrew the law.

On a utilitarian basis, laws should not be opposed with violence unless, perhaps, it is in response to existing violence. In a democracy, laws can be changed through normal legislative procedures. If laws are to be changed, the utilitarian perspective would be to assess whether the change should be made, based on whether the cost (financial and in terms of suffering or loss of life) is worth the benefits gained. Similarly, if a law benefits a minority at the expense of the majority, then that law can be opposed if it does not lead to the greatest happiness for the greatest number. For others, such as Kant, it might be right to disobey the law if it conflicts with a categorical imperative – a moral obligation, for instance, that stands in contrast to the law in question.

The purpose of punishment

'All punishment is mischief ... all punishment, in itself, is evil' (Jeremy Bentham in *Principles of Morals and Legislation*, Prometheus, 1988).

Punishments are given to ensure that laws are obeyed. Punishment is the intentional infliction of pain or suffering by a legitimate authority on those who have breached its laws. It can be inflicted by parents, employers, private organisations and, most significantly, by the state. If there were no punishments, it has been argued, citizens would not obey the law and society would collapse. In the UK, the main forms of punishment, depending on how severe the crime is, are imprisonment, fines and community services orders. In *Justice that Restores* (IVP, 2000), Charles Colson wrote:

> The primary purpose of criminal justice is to preserve order with the minimum infraction of individual liberty. Accomplishing this requires a system of law that people can agree on and that therefore possesses not just power but authority. It also requires moral standards, commonly accepted, that serve as voluntary restraints and inform conscience; an accepted understanding of what is due to – and required from – each citizen. Finally, criminal justice requires a just means to restore the domestic order when it has broken down, and a system of punishment that is redemptive.'

Punishment is seen by many as an essential part of a system that takes seriously the notions of justice, authority and law. However, the exact purpose of punishment needs to be clear and it is the state's duty to ensure that forms of punishment do not infringe the human rights of the offender. Punishment should therefore be proportional, humane and respectful to the equality and dignity of all human beings.

There are several purposes of punishment.

- **Deterrence** is about preventing or discouraging a person from doing a particular action. A punishment given to someone can also act as a deterrent – to prevent others from committing the same crime, or to deter the offender from re-offending.

- **Reform / Rehabilitation** is concerned with changing the offender's viewpoint or circumstances so that they will not re-offend. It enables them to understand what they did wrong and ensure that they do not do it

Taking it further...

In more recent times, anti-hunt protestors have campaigned against the Government's plans to make fox-hunting illegal and succeeded in delaying, for as long as a year, the final ban on the hunting with dogs.

Taking it further...

A crime is an action that is against the law and which is forbidden by the state and therefore liable to punishment. This means that certain actions – murder, theft and so on – are forbidden and the state will punish those who commit these acts.

A cell in H. M. Prison, Chelmsford

Taking it further...

Typical forms of retributive punishment include:
- corporal punishment and execution – for harm to the body
- seizing of goods or restriction of ownership, fines or restitution to the victim – for harm to property
- restriction of movement: house arrest, imprisonment, electronic tagging
- public shaming – for harm to reputation.

again. Prisons offer educational programmes that present alternative lifestyles to prisoners so they are encouraged not to return to crime. Research has suggested that keeping someone in prison without rehabilitation (and therefore without hope) may harden and demoralise prisoners and encourage them to return to crime on their release.

- **Protection** means locking someone in prison to protect the rest of society from their actions.

- **To vindicate the law** – without punishment, people will not respect and obey the law.

- **Retribution** means that those who do wrong must suffer a punishment for what they have done. The worse the crime, the harsher the punishment. Retribution is said to reinforce the values of the community, make individuals responsible for their actions and give society, and the victims of crime, a feeling of revenge.

The first four of these can be justified on utilitarian grounds – punishment is a means of minimising suffering and protecting society. The punishment imposed on one person allows many others to live in safety. The fifth one, retribution, is commonly defended on the grounds of natural justice. People tend to want revenge if they are wronged. Unlimited revenge would lead to anarchy, so the state limits and controls the amount of revenge that is taken.

In his essay *The Humanitarian View of Punishment* (*Essays and Short Pieces*, ed. Lesley Walmsley, Harper Collins, 2000) C. S. Lewis argues strongly that punishment based on desserts is part of natural law. This is the retributative theory of punishment found in Kant. For Lewis, dessert is the only proper basis for deciding what happens to criminals. He says that ideas of deterrence and rehabilitation sound merciful, but what is happening is that the criminal is losing the protection of natural law which ensures that they are punished only so far as is just, and instead is at the mercy of apparent experts who, by permission of the state, can do whatever they want to the criminal to make them behave as they see fit.

It is of fundamental importance that an offender must have committed a crime as an autonomous moral agent. In looking at the evidence, a court has to decide not only what actually happened; it is equally important to decide whether the person *intended* to commit an illegal act. This means that limits must be placed on the punishing of those who are not free moral agents – for example, those who commit crimes whilst suffering mental illness.

Taking it further...

Critics have argued that there is no evidence that reform and rehabilitation methods work and they are an expensive waste of taxpayer's money. They claim that there are more economically viable methods of punishment.

Most punishments are a mixture of all of these aspects – for instance, putting an offender in prison acts as deterrent, retribution and protection and, with the aid of education and guidance whilst in prison, offenders can be reformed. However, in the UK, nearly half of all prisoners commit crimes after they are released and are sent back to prison again.

Capital punishment

The most extreme form of punishment is capital punishment, or execution. In the UK, the death penalty was abolished in 1965 by the *Murder (Abolition of the Death Penalty) Act*; under the *European Convention on Human Rights*, execution was abolished throughout the European Union. Other nations, including the USA, still have the death penalty. It is estimated that there is one legal execution nearly every day, somewhere in the world.

Ethical theorists have long debated about whether the death penalty is an effective punishment or not. Some argue that there is an absolute right to life and that the taking of a human life by another human being can never be justified. This is a categorical imperative, for it is based not on the nature of the crime, or the needs of society, but stems from the overriding principle of the value of human life.

Others take a utilitarian approach, claiming that the loss of one criminal's life is balanced against the cost to society of keeping that person in prison for life, or the potential suffering that could result if that person is released from prison and re-offends. However, recent studies in the USA have suggested that it actually costs up to six times more to execute a prisoner than it does to keep them in prison for life. This is because the appeals process can take many years of expensive legal argument.

An electric chair, used in the USA to administer the death penalty

Arguments in support of the death penalty

- The death penalty acts as a deterrent to those thinking of committing a serious crime.
- The death penalty means that society can rid itself of its most dangerous and undesirable citizens.
- Execution is the ultimate revenge and is compensation for taking the life of another.
- Execution gives the victim's family a sense of retribution.
- Execution is cheaper than keeping a prisoner in prison for life.

Arguments against the death penalty

- In countries where the death penalty is enforced, the number of murders does not seem to drop – execution is, apparently, no deterrent.
- Many innocent people have been wrongly executed.
- Terrorists who are executed can become martyrs and this encourages more terrorism.
- Human life is very important, even sacred, and should never be taken away.

Finally, in his survey of the plight of prisoners in the USA and UK, Charles Colson (ibid.) argues for **restorative** or **relational justice**. He claims that the system of punishment has failed and that prisons are filled with many people who are not dangerous to society and are '… often hardened in their criminal disposition because of their experience'. He advocates a radical overhaul of the system of justice and imprisonment to allow the criminal to be reformed and reintegrated into the community: '… a criminal justice system that not only provides just desserts, but provides redemption as well – that recovers the wholeness of the community shattered by crime, a justice that restores'.

Taking it further...

An interesting moral point revolves around the question of whether or not a prisoner should be allowed to choose to be executed, rather than be put in prison for life. In other words, do condemned prisoners have a 'right to die'?

Index

Page numbers followed by 't' are for information in the boxes entitled 'Taking it further':
e.g., basic liberties 120t

a posteriori argument and statements 7–8, 21, 61
a priori arguments and statements 15, 61, 113
aboutness (intentionality) 46t
Abraham and Isaac 78–9, 84t
absolute ethical issues 100t
absolutism, moral 90, 95
    and situation ethics 108–9
action (*karma*) 50, 51, 53–4
actions
    and intention 53, 122
    right and wrong 90–3
after life, arguments against 44–5
    see also life after death
agapé love 109
agnosticism 29–30
America *see* United States
analogical language 67–8
analytic argument and statements 15, 15t, 61
'Angel of Mons' 9t
anicca 52
annatta ('no soul') 52
'another country' 48
Anselm, Archbishop and Saint 16, 17, 18–20,
    21–2, 26, 27
anti-realism approach, to ontological argument 26
anti-realist (non-cognitive) language 61, 112–13
antitheism 27, 35–6
Aquinas, Thomas
    on existence of God 18, 18t, 21, 21t, 74
    on law and justice 120
    on natural moral law 84, 85, 86, 87–8, 88–9
    and religious language 66, 66t, 67
    see also Summa Theologica
aretaic theories 89t
Aristotle 39, 84, 96–7, 98
atheism
    and agnosticism 29–30
    and critiques of religious belief 30
    definitions and meanings of 27–9
    and existence of God 19
    popularist critiques of 35–8
    psychological critiques of 33–5
    and religious morality 82
    sociological critiques of 30–3
    and theism 39–41
atmosphere, and religious experience 6–7
attribution, analogy of 67
Augustine 116
authority
    and natural law 88–9
    and the social contract 118–19
awareness experience 1
Ayer, A. J.
    on after life 44
    on emotivism 106–7, 110
    on religious experiences 12–13
    and verification principle 61, 62, 63

the barrier, and near-death experiences 48
basic liberties 120t

behaviourism 46t
the being of light, and near-death experiences 48
belief
    critiques of 30
        further arguments for non-existence of
            God 39
        popularist 35–8
        psychological 33–5
        sociological 30–3
    and falsification principle 64–5
    Ockham's Razor principle 39–40, 41–2
    reasons for 41
    see also atheism
Bentham, Jeremy 94, 118, 121
Bhagavad Gita 5, 50
Bible
    and after life 43t
    and arguments for existence of God 38, 39
    New Testament
        Corinthians 1 54–5
        Corinthians 2 4
        John 54
        Luke 3, 82, 91
        Matthew 84, 91t
        Revelation 56t
        Romans 84, 85, 86, 88
        Thessalonians 69
    Old Testament
        Daniel 43
        Exodus 77
        Genesis 78, 85, 117t
        Isaiah 3
        Job 54
        Judges 79, 109
        Leviticus 49t
        Psalms 19, 26, 39
        Samuel 49t
    religious language and mythology of 69–70
    see also Christianity
biblical morality, and Euthyphro dilemma 75–9
binding (obligatory) norm 85t
blik 11, 37, 64
body
    mind and soul relationships 45–7, 55
    out-of-body experiences 47
    resurrection of 54–6
Brahman 50–1
Buddha 9, 53
Buddhism
    and rebirth 50, 52–4
    and revelatory experiences 11

capital punishment 122–3
cardinal virtues 86t
categorical imperatives 92, 95
Catholic Church
    and contraception 80
    and liberation theology 33
    and revelatory experiences 11
charismatic Christianity 6–7, 11–12

Charismatic Movement 11–12
choice 93t
Christianity
    and biblical stories as myth 69t
    charismatic 6–7, 11–12
    evangelical 31–2, 36, 81–2
    and Marxism 33, 33t
    moral values of 83, 108–9, 114
    and resurrection of the body 54–6
    see also Bible
Cicero 83t
'civil liberty' 119t
civil and political rights 120
class struggle 32
Cogito, ergo sum (I think, therefore I am) 20
cognitive (realist) language 60–1, 111–12
coherence theory of truth 61t
collective unconscious 34
Colorado, New Life Church 31–2, 37
commands, ethical claims as 108
'common good', concept of 88
communism 32
community, and religion 30–1
conscience 80–1
consent, concept of 118
consequentialism 89
contemplation 2t
contingent moral values 76t
contraception 80
contract rights and duties 119
contractualism 90
conversion (dramatic) events 3
Copleston, F. C., debate with Russell 40, 74–5
'core experiences' 47
corporate experiences 2, 6
correspondence theory of truth 61t
creation/evolution debate 71t
credulity, principle of 9–10
crime and criminals 121–2, 123
crusades, miracle 6, 7
cultural relativism 114–15
cumulative argument 9

dance, and religious experience 6
Darwinism 36t
Dawkins, Richard
    on the Bible 70, 79
    objections to religious belief 35–7, 38, 57
    rejection of ontological argument 25–6
    on religious experience 3, 12, 14
    and 'virus of religion' 81–3
    *see also God Delusion; Root of All Evil?;
        Selfish Gene*
de dicto argument 18, 24t, 26
de re argument 18t, 24t
death, and post-mortem existence 43–5
    see also life after death
death penalty 122–3
decision to return, and near-death experiences 48–9
Declaration of Independence, American 119
deductive argument and reasoning 15, 26–7
democracy
    and equality 117
    and natural law 88
    and rights and duties 119
deontology 89–95, 113
Descartes, René
    dualistic view of body–mind/soul 46
    on immortality of the soul 57
    and the perfect being 20–1

deterrence 121
Dhammapada 44
dilemmas, moral 78–9
direct experience (of God) 1
discriminating norm 85t
distributive justice 118
diversity, moral 114
divine command ethics 90, 112
divine law 86
divine right 119
divorce 84
DNA 37–8
'Doctrine of Recollection' 57
double effect, principle of 87t
dramatic (conversion) events 3
dualistic view, of body and mind/soul 45, 46
duck or rabbit 10
dukkha (evil) 52
Durkheim, Emile 30–2
duty, and morality 90, 92, 93–5, 105t
    see also rights

Eastern religions 44, 46–7, 50–4
education, and religion 36
emotions, as unverifiable opinions 62
emotivism 105–10, 112
enlightenment (*moksha*) 51
epistemic distance 40
equal treatment for equals 117
equality 116–18
equivocal language 66
eschatological verification 56
eternal forms (or archetypes) 74
eternal law 86
ethical concepts 73–4
    Dawkins and 'virus of religion' 81–3
    demands of religious morality 80–1
    the Euthyphro dilemma and biblical morality
        75–9
    religion and morality 74–5
    see also morality
ethical descriptivism (naturalism) 112
ethical intuitionism (ethical non-naturalism) 111
ethical language
    emotivism 105–10
    intuitionism 104–5
    morality defined 99–101
    the naturalistic fallacy 101–4
ethical statements, verification of 62
ethical subjectivism 112
ethical theory
    deontology 89–95
    natural moral law 83–9
    virtue ethics 96–8
eudaimonia 89t, 96
Euthyphro dilemma, and biblical morality 75–9
evaluation
    of ethical claims 107–8
    of ontological argument 23–5
evangelical Christianity 31–2, 36, 81–2
    see also fundamentalism
evil
    and atheism 39
    dukkha 52
    explanations of 40
    and morality 78t
    of religion 36
evolution/creation debate 71t
evolutionary change 88t
excellence and remotion 68t

existence
    explanations of 40–1, 42
    and perfection 17–18, 20–2
existence of God
    arguments for non-existence of God 39
    moral argument for 74, 92
    proof of and atheism 29
    religious experience as proof of 7–12
    verification and falsification debates 62, 63–4
    see also religious experience
existentialism, and morality 75, 114
experience, religious *see* religious experience
extramarital sex (*zina*) 80
extremism 36–7
extrovertive mysticism 5

faith, and obedience 78–9
faith claims 36
falsification, of religious debates 62, 63–4
falsification principle 63–5
feminist theology 78
Flew, Anthony
    on atheism, deism and theism 28t, 37t, 41
    on religious experiences 13–14
    on religious language 60–1, 63–4, 79t
formulae, of Kant's laws of universalisability 92, 93
freedom, and moral choice 77, 82, 93
Freud, Sigmund 11, 33–4, 80
friends, and near-death experiences 48
function (*telos*) 96, 101t
functional explanations 30
fundamental equality 117
fundamentalism
    of Dawkins 37
    Islamic 36
    see also evangelical Christianity

general liberties 120t
generosity 92
genetics 37–8
glossolalia (speaking in tongues) 7, 12
gnostic 29
God
    definitions of 17, 20
    existence of *see* religious experience
    and justice 118
    and life after death 54–6, 58
    and morality 73, 74–7, 79
    religious statements about 62, 63, 65–6
    the Unmoved Mover 96t
The God Delusion (Dawkins) 3, 12, 14, 25, 35, 57, 70, 79t
godhatesfags website 81, 110
Golden Mean 96t, 97, 98
'good' and 'goodness' 75–6
    and justice 118
    summum bonum (complete good) 57, 82t
    use and meanings of words 100–1, 104, 111–12, 113
Good Samaritan 82
good will, and duty 92, 93, 95
graded absolutism 114
'gross body' (*sthula sharira*) 51
guilt, psychological explanations for 34
Guru Nanak 9

Haggard, Ted 31–2, 37, 81–2
happiness
    and justice 116

and natural law 89
and virtue ethics 96
hard universalism 113–14
'harm principle' 119
Heaven 58
Hell *45*, 57–8
heteronomy 92
Hick, John
    and eschatalogical verification 13t
    on life after death 44, 44t, 45t, 50, 50t, 52, 53, 57–8
        Replica Theory 55–6
    on religion and morality 74, 75
    and religious experience 11, 11t
    on religious language 63
Hinduism
    and atheism 28
    and reincarnation 50–1, 50t
Hinn, Benny 3t, 4, 6–7
historical statements, verification of 62
Hobbes, Thomas 118–19
holiness 75t
homosexuality 32, 82, 87
honour killings 80
human (or positive) law 86, 89
human life, purposes of 85–6
Human Rights, Universal Declaration of 120
humanity
    nature of 96–7
    and purpose 36
Hume, David
    and justice and equality 117
    on miracles 9
    on naturalistic fallacy 102, 103
    on non-existence of God 24, 29–30
    on religious language 66
Hume's Fork 102
'Hurrah! Boo!' theory (emotivism) 106
hymns 32t
hypothetical imperatives 92

I think, therefore I am (*Cogito, ergo sum*) 20
I-It / *I-Thou* relationships 2
illumination 2t
immortality, of the soul 56–8
imperatives, categorical and hypothetical 92, 95
impossibility mode of argument 25t
in intellectu existence 17
in re existence 17, 18
indirect experience (of God) 1
individualism 112
inductive argument 8–9
ineffability 5
inequality 117
    see also equality
intellectual virtue 96
intention, and action 53, 122
intentionality (aboutness) 46t
interpretive experience 1
intrinsic religion 34
introvertive mysticism 5
intuitionism 104–5
'is' and 'ought' 101–2
Islam
    fundamentalist 36, 81
    mysticism in 5
    Sufi dervishes 6
Islamic law (*Shariah*) 80

Jephthah the Gileadite 79

Jesus
  morality of 82, 91, 91t, 97
  resurrection of 54
Joan of Arc 9
John of the Cross, Saint 5
John Paul II, Pope 33t
judgements, moral 99
Julian of Norwich 5
Jung, Carl C. 8t, 34–5, 35t
justice
  authority and social contract 118–19
  and natural law 88–9
  and nature of law 120–1
  principles of 116–18
  and punishment 121–3
  and rights and duties 119–20

Kant, Immanuel
  on deontology 91–3, 95, 113
  on existence of God 21, 22, 23, 24
  on immortality of the soul 57–8
  on morality and existence of God 74t, 82t
  and use of reason 27t
karma (action) 50, 51, 53–4
kerygma 70
Kierkegaard, Søren 78

language
  meaning in ethical 99–101
  picture theory of language 62t
  see also ethical language
language games 26, 70–1, 105–6
  see also religious language
Last Judgement 59
Latin American Christianity 33
law(s)
  natural moral law 83–9
  nature of 120–1
  of parsimony (or simplicity) 39t, 41
  of science 62
  see also deontology; natural moral law
liberation theology 33
liberties, basic and general 120t
life after death
  body, mind and soul relationships 45–7, 55
  death and post-mortem existence 43–5
  immortality of the soul 56–8
  near-death experiences 4, 12, 46, 47–9
  parapsychology 46, 49–50
  rebirth 52–4
  reincarnation 44, 50–2
  resurrection of the body 54–6
life review, and near-death experiences 48
linga sharira ('subtle body') 51
  and reincarnation 51
Locke, John 119
logical ethical argument 108t
logical necessity 15, 16
Logical Positivists 12–13, 28, 61, 106, 110
love
  agapé 109
  as 'greatest commandment' 114

manifesting norm 85t
Marx, Karl 32–3, 116t
Marxism, and Christianity 33, 33t
materialism 46t
mathematical statements, verification of 61
maximal greatness and excellence 25
meditation, and religious experience 7

memes 37
memory, of previous life 51–2
Meno (Plato) 56–7
meta-ethics 99
Mill, John Stuart 94, 119, 120
mind, body and soul relationships 45–7, 55
miracle crusades 6, 7
miracles
  and myth 69
  and religious experience 9
modal form of argument 25t
models and qualifiers 67–8
modernism 39
moksha (enlightenment) 51
monistic deontology 90
monistic mysticism 5
monistic theories 112t
monistic view, of body and mind/soul 45–6
monotheisms, and religious behaviour 34t
Moore, G. E. 23
  on intuitionism 104–5
  on naturalistic fallacy 101, 102, 103
moral absolutism (objectivity) 113–14
moral anti-realism 112–13
moral judgements 99
moral nihilism 113
moral particularism 112–13
moral realism 111–12
moral relativism, and subjectivism 114–15
  see also objectivity
moral scepticism 112
moral statements, verification of 62
moral subjectivism 112, 115
moral virtues 96
morality
  definitions of see ethical language
  of genes 38
  religious morality 73–83
  and society 30–1
Mother Julian 5
motivation 94
Muhammad, Prophet 9
murder 85
Murder Act (UK, 1965) 122
music, and religious experience 6
Muslims see Islam; Islamic law
mystical experiences 2, 4–6
myth 69–70

nama-rupa ('name form') 52
natural moral law / natural law 83–9
natural rights 119
naturalism (ethical descriptivism) 111
naturalistic fallacy 95, 101–4
near-death experiences 4, 12, 46, 47–9
necessary existence 18
necessary moral values 76t
necessity mode of argument 25t
negation, the via negativa 65–6
New Life Church (Colorado) 31–2, 37, 81–2
New Testament see Bible
Nicomachean Ethics 97t
Nietzsche, Friedrich 82
nihilism, moral 113
9/11 terrorist attacks 36, 81
nirvana 50, 51, 52–3
noetic quality 5
non-cognitive (anti-realist) language 61, 112–13
non-cognitivism 112–13
non-propositional revelation 4

non-propositional views 112
non-rational psychological ethical argument 108t
non-theistic spirituality 45, 50
normative ethics 85t, 99t, 100t
numinous experience 1, 3

obedience
    to authority 88
    and faith 78–9
    to the law 120, 121
objectivity
    and cognitive and non-cognitive language
        111–13
    and moral absolutism 113–14
    and moral relativism and subjectivism 114–15
oceanic feeling 34
Ockham's Razor 39–40, 41–2
Old Testament see Bible
omniscience, of God 17, 19
ontic goods 86
ontological argument 15–16
    anti-realism approach 26
    content of argument 17–19
    Dawkins' rejection of 25–6
    and deductive reasoning 26–7
    Descartes and the perfect being 20–1
    evaluation of 23–5
    and language games 26
    objections to argument 21–3
    strengths and weaknesses of 19–20
ontological reduction 37–8
open question argument 103
'ought' and 'is' 101–2
out-of-body experiences 47

Parable of the Celestial City (Hick) 63
Parable of the Gardener (Wisdom) 14t, 64, 64t
Parable of the Partisan and the Stranger (Mitchell)
        64–5
parapsychology 46, 49–50
parsimony (or simplicity), law of 39t, 41
particularism, moral 112–13
passivity 5
paternalism 89t, 120
Paul, Saint
    conversion of 3, 9
    on life after death 54t
    on moral law 84, 85, 86, 88
peace, and near-death experiences 47
perfect being 20–1
perfect island 22
perfection, and existence 17–18, 20–2
personal unconscious 34
Phaedo (Plato) 56, 57, 75t
philosophical behaviourism 46
picture theory of language 62t
Plato
    and eternal forms (or archetypes) 74
    the Euthyphro dilemma 75–9
    on immortality of the soul 47t, 56–7
    on justice 116, 118t
    and moral absolutism 113
pluralistic theories 112t
political authority 88–9
political and civil rights 120
Poll Tax (Community Charge) 120t
positive (or human) law 86, 89
possibility mode of argument 25t
post-mortem existence, and death 43–5
postmodernism, language game theory 70–1

prayer, and religious experience 3, 7
prescriptive language 100–1, 112
prima facie duties 93–5, 105t
principle of credulity 10
principle of testimony 9–10
profane, and sacred 31t
projective explanations 30, 33–4
projective religion 34
promises 92t
proportionalism 86–7
proportionality, analogy of 67
propositional revelation 4
Proslogion (Anselm) 16, 19, 27
protection 122
psychological critiques, of religion 33–5
psychological issues
    arguments to explain religious experience 3,
        11, 13
    need for religious explanations 40
punishment
    law and justice 121–3
    and natural law 89
purgation 2t
purpose
    and humanity 36
    telos 96, 101t

qualia 46t
qualifiers and models 67–8
quasi-realism 112
quasi-sensory experience 1

rational psychological ethical argument 108t
rational thought 96
rationalism 16t, 39
realist (cognitive) language 60–1, 111–12
reason
    and deductive argument 15, 26–7
    and morality 85, 92, 96
rebirth 46, 50, 51t, 52–4
redemption 88
reductio ad absurdum 16, 22
reform 121–2
regenerative experience 1
rehabilitation 121–2
reincarnation 44, 46, 50–2
relationships
    of body, mind and soul 45–7
    and experience of God 2
relative ethical issues 100t
relatives, and near-death experiences 48
relativism, moral, and subjectivism 114–15
    see also objectivity
religion
    and morality 74–5
    popularist critiques of 35–8
    psychological critiques of 33–5
    sociological critiques of 30–3
religious experience 1–3
    factors leading to 6–7
    meaning and significance of 12–14
    as proof of God's existence 7–10
        arguments against 10–12
    types of 3–6
religious language 60–1
    language game theory 70–1
    use of religious language 66–70
    verification and falsification debate 61–5
    the via negativa 65–6
religious morality 73–9

demands of 80–1
  and the 'virus of religion' 81–3
remotion and excellence 68t
Replica Theory 55–6
reproduction, human 87, 88
The Republic (Plato) 116, 118t
restorative justice 118, 123
result, of action 53
resurrection of the body 54–6
retributive punishment 122
return to life, and near-death experiences 49
revelatory experiences 2, 3–4, 11–12
rights 90, 94
  to die 123t
  duties and justice 119–20, 123
rituals, psychological explanations for 34
The Root of All Evil? (TV broadcast) (Dawkins) 35, 36–7, 44, 81
rules *see* deontology; natural moral law
ruling classes 32
Russell, Bertrand
  debate with Copleston 40, 74–5
  on life after death 44, 46
  on moral judgements 108
  and ontological argument for existence of God 16, 23, 24, 24t
  on resurrection of the body 55

sacred, and profane 31t
samskaras (impressions) 51
Sarah (wife of Abraham) 78
scepticism, moral 112
scientific critiques 37–8, 39
secondary precepts 85–6
seeing-as 10
The Selfish Gene (Dawkins) 35, 38
September 11 terrorist attacks 36, 81
7/7 terrorist attacks 36, 81
sexuality, and spirituality 34
Shariah (Islamic law) 80
simplicity (or parsimony), law of 39t, 41
situation ethics 82, 108–9
social contract theories 88, 118–19
social equality 117
social harmony 116
social immortality 58t
society
  justice and equality 117–18
  religion in 30–3
soul
  body and mind relationships 45–7, 55
  and concepts of after life 44, 50–1
  immortality of 56–8
  and rebirth 52
  and reincarnation 51
speaking in tongues (glossolalia) 7, 12
spiritualism 49t
Spiritualist Movement 49–50
spirituality
  non-theistic 45, 50
  and sexuality 34
sthula sharira ('gross body') 51
subjectivism, and moral relativism 114–15
  see also objectivity
'subtle body' (*linga sharira*) 51
suffering, and morality 77–8, 79
Sufism 5, 6
Summa Theologica (Aquinas) 55, 58, 66, 84, 88, 89
  Fourth Way, *The Gradation of Things* 74t

summum bonum (complete good) 57, 82t
Sunday Schools 32t
super-ego 33
Swinburne, Richard
  on atheism and belief 40, 41t
  and falsification principle 65
  on life after death 49
  on religion and morality 76t
  on religious experiences 8, 9–10, 13, 13t
symbolic language 68–70
synthetic statements 61–2

taxation
  Community Charge 120t
  and equality 117t
telos (purpose or function) 96, 101t
Teresa of Avila, Saint 1, 3
terrorism 36, 38, 81, 119t
testimonies, from USA 2
testimony, principle of 9–10
theism
  and atheism 39–41
  and resurrection of the body 56
  see also non-theistic spirituality
theistic mysticism 5
Tibetan Book of the Dead 4
Toronto Blessing 2, 6
totalitarian rights and duties 120
transciency 5
'transitional error' 21
truth
  coherence and correspondence theories of 61
  and myth 70
tsunami (Dec 2005) 35
tunnel and the light, and near-death experiences 48

the unconscious 34
unequal treatment 117
United States
  Christian fundamentalism in 31–2, 81
  Declaration of Independence 119
Universal Declaration of Human Rights (1948) 120
universal moral code 113–14
universalisability, principle of 92–3, 95
univocal language 66
Unmoved Mover 96t
utilitarian
  justification for punishment 122, 123
  rights and duties 120, 121
utilitarianism 89, 94, 113t, 118

verification
  of ethical claims 106–7
  of religious language 61–5
verification principle 61–3
via negativa 65–6
vices (deadly sins) 86t
Vienna Circle 61, 62
vinnana 52
virtue ethics 86t, 89t, 96–8
virus, religion as 36, 37, 81–3

Wesley, John 3
Westboro Baptist Church 81, 110
Witch of Endor 49t
Wittgenstein, Ludwig 10, 26, 59, 62t, 70–1, 105–6
women, and equality 117t

zina (extramarital sex) 80